D1257410

Modern Authoritarianism

Modern Authoritarianism

A Comparative Institutional Analysis

AMOS PERLMUTTER

New Haven and London
Yale University Press

Published with assistance from the foundation
established in memory of Philip Hamilton McMillan
of the Class of 1894, Yale College.

Copyright © 1981 by Yale University.
All rights reserved.
This book may not be reproduced, in whole
or in part, in any form (beyond that
copying permitted by Sections 107 and 108
of the U.S. Copyright Law and except by
reviewers for the public press), without
written permission from the publishers.

Designed by James J. Johnson
and set in Aster Roman type.
Printed in the United States of America by
The Vail-Ballou Press, Binghamton, N.Y.

Library of Congress Cataloging in Publication Data

Perlmutter, Amos.
    Modern authoritarianism.

    Bibliography: p.
    Includes index.
    1. Authoritarianism. 2. State, The. 3. Social
structure. 4. Political socialization. I. Title.
HM271.P46   306'.2   81–3403
ISBN 0–300–02640–4   AACR2

10   9   8   7   6   5   4   3   2   1

TO THE SPECIAL WOMEN:
My mother, Berta Perlmutter
My friend, Rosanne Druian

Contents

Apologia Writ Large

"When we deal with complex political phenomena we find ourselves circumstanced like intelligent laymen bereft of comprehensive theory."*

Apples and pears are not identical. Nazism cannot be equated with praetorianism nor bolshevism with fascism, but they can be compared. I offer here a synthesis and, I hope, a theoretically suggestive typology of the most conspicuous political fact of modern times—authoritarianism. In the absence of a general theory in the social and political sciences, the best that can be said for any such preliminary classification, continues Gregor, is that "similarities in political and social science are generally sought out to support some interpretive argument, or as the basis for empirical generalizations. The business of social science, in fact, is the searching out of just such similarities—precisely to serve such purposes—for social science is predicated on a regularity analysis of complex and seemingly unique sequences of events. The fact that everything in the natural and social universe is, in some sense, unique is not enough to discredit the effort to identify, isolate, code, and employ significant similarities. Every tree and shrub, every insect and fish, every nation, and every human being, is unique in a clear and indisputable sense. But botany and entomology, ichthyology, and political and social science proceed to categorize, classify, and generalize on the basis of what are conceived to be fruitful similarities."†

*A. James Gregor, *Italian Fascism and Developmental Dictatorship* (Princeton, N.J.: Princeton University Press, 1979), p. 301.
†Ibid., pp. 300–01.

In this book, I try to identify and distinguish the political and structural behavior of modern authoritarian regimes. This does not mean that the links I establish will answer all or even most of the questions that students of authoritarian regimes may ask, but given the many first-rate empirical monographs on authoritarian regimes, the time is ripe to clarify our understanding of modern authoritarianism.

I am aware of the price paid for synthesis and for analytic comprehensiveness. I am especially sensitive to the opinions of historians, who may feel that history has been reduced to political processes. I also acknowledge the concerns of methodologically oriented political scientists, some of whom are more concerned with methodological procedures than with political explanations and therefore are dubious about the value of a comparative and theoretical approach. The canvas is wide, and some significant details will unfortunately be lost; I have, however, found it worthwhile to study the political dynamics of modern authoritarianism in this way. My study has yielded a reward that I hope others will share with me. I hope also that others will refine this preliminary classification.

Preface and Acknowledgments

The twentieth century is the age of political authoritarianism. Its most influential political movements and ideologies are not liberalism and democracy, but Marxism and fascism. Its most conspicuous political innovations include the unopposed single party, the party-state, political police, the politburo, revolutionary command councils, storm troops, political youth movements, cadres and gulags, propaganda machinery, and concentration camps. The dictators of authoritarian states are among the most prominent political men of the age: Lenin, Stalin, Mussolini, Hitler, Himmler, Mao Tse-tung, Ho Chi Minh, Franco, Salazar, Nasser, and Perón. The political revolution of the twentieth century is represented by mass participation and mass mobilization. It is the age of collective political behavior and of organizations.

Much has been written on modern authoritarian political systems. Scholars in all of the social sciences, journalists, and novelists have been fascinated and repelled by dictatorships based on mass mobilization, political repression, and military domination. Political scientists and psychologists continue to examine the social and personal impulses that govern the development and structure of modern authoritarian systems. Philosophers and ideologists have invented a new political concept—totalitarianism—and have extended its implications into social and political theory. Historians of Nazi Germany, especially, are having a field day: documents and research material abound. There has been a recent outpouring of biographies, psychohistories, films, and analyses of Adolf Hitler, the most repellent of modern tyrants, and of Joseph Stalin, who came close to equaling him in brutality. There is also a burgeoning literature on developing countries, practically all of which are authoritarian states.

More has been written on the causes behind the evolution and development of modern authoritarian regimes than on liberalism, democracy, and socialism. This literature is replete with interpretations of totalitarianism, which are offered as overviews of the modern authoritarian state. It also tries to explain the origins of totalitarian ideology. Rather than lump political phenomena together as in a totalitarian model, I will emphasize the relationships among the regime, the state, the party, and auxiliary political institutions as the factors of modern authoritarian political behavior.

Authoritarian political systems are sustained and protected by specially designed political entities that I call parallel and auxiliary structures. Parallel structures have a dual function: to accomplish seizure of power (*Machtergreifung*) and to protect the regime in critical times from internal opposition or perceived threats. The SS, Red Guards, and similar parapolice and paramilitary structures are examples. Auxiliary structures commonly evolve from political projects of restricted life spans into sometimes permanent and distinctive political structures of modern authoritarianism. In fact, one characteristic of a long-lived authoritarian system is the survival and resilience of these institutions and their ability to assume the functions of political mobilization, control, or propaganda. A regime can establish legitimacy not only through the use of symbols but, more importantly, through these auxiliary political structures.

Much has been written on the role of the totalitarian party or what in effect is the monopolistic party. The totalitarian party model adequately explains the Bolshevik party-state. It is a less potent explanation for the Nazi regime from the time Hitler was securely saddled in power in 1934. It fails altogether to explain the political behavior of the corporate-praetorian authoritarian system, which includes nonparty regimes. In Franco's and Salazar's corporatist states, the party did not play a key role in securing legitimacy and maintaining order. A comparative analysis of the political structures and instruments typical of totalitarian models of authoritarian regimes and those of more general political models has not yet been made. The current totalitarian explanation of modern authoritarian regimes is incomplete because it does not go beyond analyzing the origins and ideological purposes of modern totalitarian movements. A description of tendencies is not sufficient to explain the success of authoritarianism; the *dynamics* of modern authoritarianism must be analyzed and explained. It is my contention that the relations between the principal political instruments of modern authoritarian regimes—the single dominating party, parallel and auxiliary structures, and the state—will explain both the dynamics and the political longevity of authoritarian systems.

A comparative typology and functional analysis of modern authoritarian regimes will reveal considerably more about the working of authoritarian systems than about their origins. The totalitarian school has concentrated on explaining *why* totalitarianism exists; I prefer to explain *where* these regimes are going and *how* they actually work. To do this, it is necessary to set aside ideological-psychological explanations of the sources of totalitarianism, which often concentrate on the metaphysical origins of mass manipulation and propaganda techniques. An analysis of the dynamics of authoritarian political instruments not only entails causal explanations of the phenomenon, but it can also explain the similarities and differences between various types of authoritarianism. I therefore prefer a typology based on the dynamics of political structures to one based on the dynamics of totalitarian control.

No book is written by one person. This synthesis is derived from a multitude of sources. I am grateful to historians, philosophers, political scientists, psychologists, sociologists, and others who have labored in the vineyard of authoritarianism. All are present in my footnotes. I am in debt to Howard Wiarda of the University of Massachusetts for carefully going over an earlier draft and to Juan J. Linz of Yale University, who gave me much time and good advice even though there are still some profound disagreements on the nature of modern authoritarianism. Several of my friends and colleagues will find how useful their ideas and advice were: Samuel

P. Huntington and Richard Pipes of Harvard, Seymour Martin Lipset of Stanford, Richard Betts of The Brookings Institution, Theda Skocpol of Harvard, and Roman Kolkowicz of the University of California, Los Angeles.

To Barbara Majeur of Stanford, to copyeditor Floyd Tomkins, and to Gary Tischler of American University I am most grateful for their editorial help. To Yale University Press, my home where my third book is being published, and particularly to Maura D. Shaw Tantillo and Charlotte Dihoff for efficiency and good care of the manuscript, I owe special thanks. Last and not least I thank Senior Editor Marian Neal Ash, without whom this book would not exist.

AMOS PERLMUTTER
Washington, D.C.

May 1981

CHAPTER ONE

Definitions and Models

Historical Autocracy, Tyranny, and Authoritarianism

The conventional definitions of autocracy, tyranny, and authoritarianism are quite similar; however, autocracy and tyranny describe the nature of the ruler while authoritarianism refers to the nature of the regime and the structure of its management. Autocracy may be defined as rule by a single person wielding absolute executive power. Autocratic government contains no legal provision for limitation of powers, accountability, or orderly succession. Rule is arbitrary and maintained by force. Tyranny is virtually synonymous, being the arbitrary government of no king (instituted) by law. Tyrannical authority is secured by conquest and maintained by fear. An authoritarian regime may be a collective dictatorship, an oligarchy, or a military government. The term connotes collective rule, though supreme power may be vested in a single person as it was in Rome, for example, when one tribune temporarily assumed unlimited power.

Significantly, definitions of autocracy assume the lack of a permanent and institutionalized power structure. In this respect they are politically incomplete because authority so defined is identified with personal leadership, that is, domination-submission relationships, and is not related to institutional, superordinate-subordinate relationships.[1]

Tyranny took its classical form in the seventh and sixth cen-

1. On the relation between leadership and authority, see Robert Bierstadt, "The Problem of Authority," in *Freedom and Control in Modern Society*, ed. Morroe Berger et al. (New York: Van Nostrand, 1954), pp. 71–72; and Robert Dahl, *Modern Political Analysis*, 3d ed. (Englewood Cliffs, N.J.: Prentice Hall, 1976), pp. 25–53.

1

turies B.C.; *tyrannoi* ("tyrants") meant rulers possessing great wealth. In the fifth and fourth centuries B.C. tyranny connoted preeminence and ostentatious display. Only with the rise of democracy did the pejorative connotation obtain that tyrants were rulers without a legitimate (usually hereditary) claim to office. They could, however, institute a hereditary line of succession and thus legitimate their power. Tyrants could court and reward popular support and were at times favored by the peasantry because they divided up big estates.[2] Tyranny, however, meant personal and noninstitutionalized rule; whatever popularity it achieved went to the tyrant, not to the institution. A tyrant's power ordinarily did not remain intact for more than two generations and was not sustained by followers.

There is a clear distinction between modern and early notions of authoritarianism. The early version was rule by the few in the name of the few; modern authoritarianism is rule by the few in the name of the many. Modern authoritarianism is further distinguished by the scope and type of political support, control, mobilization, and ideology. I prefer to use authoritarianism rather than autocracy in describing modern examples and to use autocratic regimes rather than dictatorship, which is a modern term and connotes collectivity. Parenthetically, it is significant that the *Encyclopedia of the Social Sciences*, 1931–1933 edition, notes that "the modern dictator never omits to win popular support."[3] Modern authoritarianism depends on political elites, on popular support, and on political mobilization, however limited, exclusionary, and restrictive, but above all on specialized political structures and institutions.

The Modern State: Autonomy

The autonomy and centrality of the state is the most important concept in modern politics. As William Doyle notes, "Before 1789

2. Chester Starr, *A History of the Ancient World*, 2d ed. (New York: Oxford University Press, 1974), pp. 212–13.
3. *Encyclopedia of the Social Sciences*, (New York: Macmillan, 1931), s.v. "Dictatorship."

the idea of the state, as we understand it now, [as an autonomous political and sovereign unit] was only half formulated."[4] Most states at that time, however, were geographically very small and were concentrated in Germany, Switzerland, and, to a lesser extent, Italy.

Montesquieu, in an early analysis, classified forms of state government as monarchical, republican, or despotic according to the degree of a state's autonomy. In republics, the state was dependent on society. The monarchical state, represented by royalty, was sometimes coequal with the aristocratic classes. Only in despotic systems was the state autonomous, that is, totally independent of society. For Montesquieu, the model despotic states were Russia and Ottoman Turkey.[5] In czarist Russia the state was omnipotent, while in the Ottoman Empire the ruling institution was unrelated to society.[6] Characteristically, the machinery of the despotic state, such as the bureaucracy and the military, was the measure of its power. Thus the state's autonomy depended on control over these instruments of domination and increased as the state machinery expanded in power and presence.

Otto Hintze, the German historian, writes, "All state organization was originally military organization, organization for war."[7] Only in the nineteenth century the "military organization was finally brought into harmony with the political, constitutional principle of the predominance of the [Prussian] crown."[8] In analyzing social revolution, Theda Skocpol points out that the autonomy of the modern state is based on domination of the state by the politico-military class. Explaining the relationship between social revolutions and the state, she writes, "The state properly conceived is no mere arena in which socioeconomic struggles are fought out.

4. William Doyle, *The Old European Order, 1660–1800* (London: Oxford University Press, 1978), p. 221.

5. Ibid.

6. See Richard Pipes, *Russia: The Old Regime* (New York: Scribners, 1974); and H. A. R. Gibb and Harold Bowen, *Islamic Society and the West* (London: Oxford University Press), vol. 1, part 1 (1950) and vol. 1, part 2 (1957).

7. Felix Gilbert, ed., *The Historical Essays of Otto Hintze* (New York: Oxford University Press, 1975), p. 181.

8. Ibid., p. 210.

It is, rather, a set of administrative, policing, and military organizations headed, and more or less well coordinated by an executive authority."[9] Contrary to what orthodox Marxists would say, the state is not an epiphenomenal structure but a tremendously significant independent structure.

Modern authoritarianism has greatly enhanced the autonomy of the state. The despotic state has become a populist, modernizing, and mobilizing entity, and this transformation of Montesquieu's states is connected with the social and ideological revolution of the twentieth century. Authoritarian states have undergone social transformations, some partial and others revolutionary. The creation of new political structures and institutions to accommodate social revolution has also strengthened the state. It has become more sophisticated, employing parallel and auxiliary political structures to enhance its own authority, scope of domination, and level of control. State building, the outcome of social revolutions, also means a revolution in the conception, structure, and behavior of the state. As Skocpol observes, "Social revolutions, moreover, have changed state structures as much or more [sic] as they have changed class relations, societal values, and social institutions."[10]

This study deals with regimes that enlarged and changed the modern state structure, its autonomy, and its mechanisms of control. They accomplished this at the expense of society and its development, even though increased and concentrated state power was intended to surpass old state systems in development and modernization. The myth of the state as society's sole salvation—its striving for autonomy and expansion at the expense of social and economic resources—is the story of the modern authoritarian state.

The new despotism, with its power over the population and the nation, merely enhanced the state. It did not necessarily reinforce the movements that originally brought about the transformation of society and established the state.

9. Theda Skocpol, *State and Social Revolution: A Comparative Analysis of France, Russia, and China* (Cambridge: At the University Press, 1979), p. 29.

10. Ibid.

Political Centralization by the Political Elite

The model for all modern authoritarian political structures is the state-controlled, centralized, and hierarchical bureaucracy. Under modern authoritarianism, no autonomous political, economic, social, cultural, or ideological organizations can exist outside of the state.

The authoritarian state relies on an altered Marxian paradigm: the state owns the means of organization. In the authoritarian system domination implies exclusive command over the means of mobilizing a majority of the population to support the regime; it also means the state is essential to every organization because it provides the facilities necessary for sustenance and survival.

There is, however, an additional political dynamic that characterizes the authoritarian state and clearly differentiates it from other types: the linkage between the political elite and the state. The political elite commands the state, mans its organizations, puts into effect the state's policies, and mobilizes its resources. This elite is distributed among key political structures, which vary from one type of modern authoritarian state to another.

There are several types of authoritarian regimes. Some are institutionalized—communist and fascist systems are examples— and the others are not—for instance, corporatist and praetorian regimes. The relationships between the political elite, the state, and other principal political institutions vary. In the communist system, the party is theoretically the sole political entity; the state, the army, and the political police are its structural partners. The party and its elite are dominant both theoretically and in fact. They pervade and politicize the society and link the party to the state and the state to the society. In most instances, the party is hegemonic; the political elite is distributed among all of the highly centralized, bureaucratic, and exclusive organizations. The party, however, remains the reservoir of political power, personnel, and other resources.

In authoritarian systems a struggle for power ordinarily emerges between competing elites. In the organizational, oligopolistic world of the authoritarian state, elites compete to dominate the hegemonic political structure: the party in the communist system, the military in the praetorian system, and the grand corporatist structures in the fascist and corporatist systems. Party monopoly in the communist model, for instance, is continually challenged by competing institutions and their elites, whose interests sometimes diverge from those of the prevailing party elite.

Eventually, at least in the communist authoritarian model, this oligopolistic competition results in a symbiotic relationship that actually intensifies the drive for hegemony. The existence of an opposition that may consolidate itself usually forces both functions to cooperate and to overlook their conflicting orientations. The ruling political elite, which is distributed among all structures, encourages this cooperation. The lines of cooperation, however, are sometimes more vertical within subordinate institutions than horizontal between members of the ruling elite.

In the nazi system, the party elite, the state bureaucracy, and the political police all claimed exclusive and monopolistic domination of the state. Unlike the communist elite, only Hitler and the top Nazi hierarchy dominated the state's central political structures. The nazi model was certainly modern authoritarian in its organization and political support, yet, unlike the Soviet state, it did not eliminate all the political structures and elites of the regime. Hitler's domination substituted for effective Nazi control.

Germany had a highly educated and professional political class but could be governed by a less educated and less skilled Nazi elite. But, while the Nazi elite that infiltrated the Foreign Office were not eminent diplomats, the SS elite in the military was made up of distinguished professional soldiers. However, the SS failed to purge the military of its traditional leaders, and it continued to be dominated by a cohesive Prussian elite. Plainly, the Nazi party never established itself as an exclusive reservoir of political power. Perhaps the Nazi political elite simply lacked time to gain the upper hand. Certainly Hitler's war effort catapulted the military, the industrialists, and the state bureaucracy into the position of essential and thus invulnerable state institutions.

In fascist, corporatist, and praetorian systems, the state and the other political structures are unstable, inefficient, and generally weak. The elite has no cohesion and cannot attain the exclusivity it has in communist systems, nor does it dominate any hegemonic political structure suitable for establishing itself in political supremacy. The Fascist elite, however, had more control than elites in the corporatist and praetorian systems, where no formal or informal institutional rules make the organizational elites dominant.

In corporatist and praetorian systems, however, the military elite serves as the reservoir of political power and mobilizes the political organizations and the state. Ordinarily, the military elite is untrained in politics and lacks political skills; party and state bureaucracies are superior in both respects. Yet the military's proximity to political power motivates it to become involved in politics. In the absence of an authoritative political elite, sustaining political structures, and a stable political order, the corporate orientation of the military impels it to intervene.[11]

The modern authoritarian model is an exclusive, centralist political organization populated and dominated by an oligarchic political elite. Although the political elite comprises the leaders of the centralized political organization and the political organization furnishes the structures the elite uses to enforce its domination and to achieve its political and organizational goals, the linkage is not tautological but parallel and simultaneous. Both—elites and political organizations—are necessary conditions for modern authoritarianism.

Authoritarian Domination, Collective Behavior, and Political Intervention

The political behavior of modern authoritarian regimes is the result of the interaction among their internal political structures and institutions. These regimes are characterized by repression, intol-

11. For a persuasive argument on politics and corporatism in the military, see Amos Perlmutter, *The Military and Politics in Modern Times* (New Haven: Yale University Press, 1977).

erance, encroachment on the private rights and freedom of citizens, and limited autonomy for nonstatist interest groups. It is the predominance of certain types of political institutions and procedures and the distinctive behavior of their rulers that distinguishes authoritarian from democratic regimes.

To say that authoritarian political systems are undemocratic does not explain their behavior adequately. Only in the broadest sense are all nondemocratic systems authoritarian. My concern is the degree to which a given system is more or less authoritarian. Authoritarian systems should be analyzed along a continuum; apples should be compared with apples.

My major aim here is to identify the types of political structures, institutions, and methods required to create and sustain an authoritarian political system, and to ascertain the *relative* and *different* distribution of these necessary appurtenances and the significance of any variations.

The function of the authoritarian state or regime is to politicize and bureaucratize society at the expense of cultural, social, and intellectual resources. It seeks both vertical and horizontal domination. The major preoccupation of the *officials* of the authoritarian system is to establish institutions that provide or facilitate intelligence gathering, domination and control of politics, instruments and practices that inhibit autonomous social action, politicizing controlled social action, bureaucratization of society and political structures, creation of administrative and punitive instruments, regulation and supervision of culture, and control over its own instruments of repression.

To politicize society according to its own ideal, the authoritarian state must destroy or integrate existing political institutions and structures. It therefore establishes hierarchical, bureaucratic, and autonomous political structures designed to subvert or destroy target institutions and turn newly created entities into instruments of political domination. In revolutionary situations, the old regime and its institutions may already have been swept away, making this task easier. The decisive point is that new authoritarian institutions subordinate politics to policy.

There are three major instruments for the intervention, penetration, and supervision of collective and institutional behavior whose functions are delineated, but integrative: the single authoritarian party, the bureaucratic-military complex (the corporative system), and, above all, the parallel and auxiliary structures of domination, mobilization, and control. These instruments are employed differently by different types of modern authoritarian regimes, allowing regimes to be classified accordingly. Each type of authoritarian regime, while employing all three, will favor one instrument over the others. One regime may dispense with the use of the single party and employ the military as the instrument of domination. Another type would make extensive use of the political police, an auxiliary instrument, at the expense of the single party and the military. Another might enhance the patrimonial-clientalist and corporatist groups at the expense of party and state. Still another might use revolutionary guards—an auxiliary instrument—to replace the party.

Thus the different types of authoritarian regimes are distinguished by the ways these instruments are employed. The relationships among the three (or the absence of one of them, as in non-party regimes) produce different types of authoritarian political behavior. Since all authoritarian regimes compete for political support, authoritarian systems are also differentiated according to the priority each instrument is given. Thus, the bolshevik model's principal political instrument is the party. The nazi model relies on the police and propaganda. The corporate-praetorian authoritarian type relies on the state bureaucracy and the military for support.

Modern authoritarianism manifests itself in the nexus of party, state, and parallel-auxiliary structures. The relationships among the three are symbiotic but shift to form partnerships and dependencies (not always equal) among them. The parallel and auxiliary structures also link party and state to the authoritarian regime. Auxiliary structures could temporarily parallel the structures of the state; parallel structures, however, parallel or surrogate structures of the party and the state (the military and the bureaucracy, for example). Both parallel and auxiliary structures can become enormous bureaucracies with both party and state functions. In the

Soviet and Chinese communist regimes, the party began as a
parallel structure. In the Nazi and Fascist regimes, auxiliary structures became prominent, since the Nazi and Fascist parties failed
to parallel the state functions they assumed or party functions they
established after the seizure of power.

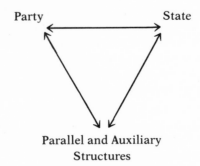

Parallel and Auxiliary
Structures

   Once I establish the political and structural requirements for
modern authoritarianism, a typology of authoritarian political
structures will emerge that realistically explains the political behavior and dynamics of all modern authoritarian political systems.
It is imperative that a student of comparative politics identify the
types of political support and the methods of securing support and
legitimacy in different systems. Authoritarian systems require different methods of securing support, legitimacy, and order than are
found in democratic-liberal political systems. For that purpose the
authoritarian system innovated instruments of domination,
mobilization, and influence—parallel and auxiliary structures.
   Without exception, from the Bolsheviks to the autocratic
praetorians of Uganda and Libya, from the Nazis to Franco,
Salazar, Nasser, and Perón, modern autocracies and authoritarian
regimes seek popular legitimacy and support. Analysis of their nature, structure, and political dynamics must be focused on this
axiomatic requirement of political support and on changes in political structures, institutions, and procedures to obtain it.
   Authoritarian regimes cannot tolerate the competing procedures, institutions, and structures that secure political legitimacy
in more open societies. Therefore, they invented two major instru-

ments for capturing political support: the all-inclusive, mobilizational political party and the restricted, nonparty, executive council of a military ruling group. Alternatively, such regimes rely on support from modern elites: bureaucrats, managers, technocrats, and the military. No authoritarian modern regime can survive politically if it lacks instruments of mobilization or the critical support of these modern elites. The central importance of political and state-oriented elites is a dominant theme of modern authoritarianism and a primary factor in the political behavior of the instruments of mobilization. Politicized elites are instrumental in domination, mobilization and control.

Although either the single mobilizational or military party functions as an instrument of domination, the major innovation of a century of authoritarian political development is the creation of three types of auxiliary structures: political police for political and societal harassment, praetorian guards (military squads, brigands), and militant subelite groups (Red Guards, youth and student movements). These instruments are necessary to sustain and protect the authoritarian regime; they secure the integrity of the regime, the lives of elites, and the survival of the party.

It is the nature of oligarchical and authoritarian systems to depend on extrapolitical and paramilitary structures to defend it both internally and externally. In regimes that derive their legitimacy from and are organized around single mobilizational parties, the most important auxiliary structure almost always is the party's praetorian guard, as in the Soviet and in early Nazi experience, which protects the party from its internal enemies. In authoritarian single-party states, the political police is not always distinguished clearly from the party. In the Soviet Union, for example, it has become a very important party apparatus, the CPSU Control Commission. An auxiliary structure also may become autonomous and compete successfully with the party for supremacy, as occurred in Nazi Germany.

Under autocratic dictatorships, the function of the political police is restricted, being largely confined to protecting the dictator and the oligarchs. Since most modern autocratic dictatorships are military regimes, the relationship between the military oligarchy and the political police is not the same as in the mobilizational and revolutionary types. In praetorian regimes, the political police generally are subordinate to the military dictator or junta that was responsible for the coup. The police usually are not very significant politically and certainly are not autonomous.

Both autocracies and authoritarian regimes frequently use paramilitary organizations (militia, rovers, brigand groups) to support the regime, usually temporarily. The mobilizational single-party regime, however, usually institutionalizes instruments of control and uses the military and the police to protect the state. In less institutionalized autocratic and praetorian regimes, paramilitary organizations are employed more frequently for political suppression.

Parallel and Auxiliary Structures

Parallel structures parallel the historical functions of the state and the requirements of the single party; they are designed to support authoritarian political domination. Auxiliary structures are somewhat different. Designed as instruments of control, they are most conspicuous as instruments of mobilization, penetration, and police. Parallel structures are executive and policy information institutions, while auxiliary structures serve to exert control: police, surveillance and penetration, and destruction of the authoritarian regime's enemies are essential functions. Auxiliary structures in the seizure of power (revolutionary guards, terror squads, special troops) are essential for the annihilation of internal (to the party or movement) and external foes. Parallel structures before seizure of power represent the embryo of the authoritarian political party. Parallel structures also define the relationship between the instruments of domination and the instruments of control.

As noted earlier, modern authoritarian regimes, especially the mobilization-revolutionary types, devised political institutions whose functions, which paralleled those of their classical-historical counterparts, were to buttress autocracy, widen control, and establish and protect executive power. These structures play key roles before seizures of power because then they are the revolutionary movement's only political instruments. After the seizure of power, they are used to legitimize and institutionalize the new regime.

It is most significant that the dominant elite, the most authoritative political class, emerges from and controls the parallel and auxiliary structures in the period preceding the seizure of power. As we shall see later, parallel structures play more significant roles in highly institutionalized authoritarian regimes than in noninstitutionalized regimes. In some cases, parallel structures become appendages to the existing political and bureaucratic structure.

Ideally, parallel structures form a pyramid of power in which each state and societal structure and geographical unit is directly controlled by a functionally equivalent unit in the party. The bolshevik system is exemplary in this respect. For instance, the Military Party Administration (MPA) controls the military, the Central Control Commission controls the police, and other bodies dominate all cultural, economic, and professional arenas. Their function, once more, is the party's penetration, domination, and control of society and of the state. The Nazi *Gleichschaltung* (political coordination) system suffered by comparison to the Soviet parallel structure.

Parallel structures may, alternatively, be no more than project-oriented groups of activists that fulfill their roles during the seizure of power and then retreat (usually unwillingly) to become auxiliary appendages of the regime. Thus, Nazi parapolice and paramilitary structures like the SA and SS duplicated functions of traditional law enforcement agencies, served as control instruments and, though they intervened infrequently, infuriated the modern military and bureaucracy. They did not retreat. They were integrated into the Hitlerian system. Similarly, Nazi, Fascist, and Bolshevik youth movements represented invasions of the community's educational and cultural arrangements, which historically had been considered the province of the private sector.

The Gleichschaltung policy was meant to ape the Soviet concept of party leadership in state and society, which would oblige economic, social, or professional organizations to accept Nazi party members as their leaders.[12]

12. Dietrich Orlow, *The History of the Nazi Party, 1933–1945* (Pittsburgh: University of Pittsburgh Press, 1973), p. 29n.

While the Soviets institutionalized political coordination through the party by employing parallel structures to dominate state and society, in Nazi Germany the party failed to incorporate into a highly industrialized society its forerunners, the Gauleiters and the Alte Kämpfers ("Old Fighters"). This failure of political coordination in Nazi Germany demonstrated the political incompetence of the Nazi middle and lower echelons.

The Leninist system by contrast made the parallel structures into permanent institutions that coordinated the party, the state, and society. Parallel structures became fundamental to the symbiosis of party and state in the Leninist system.

The most glaring contrast of relationships between party, state, and parallel and auxiliary structures is between those of the Leninist and the nazi systems, especially in their uses of parallel and auxiliary structures. The KGB—the Soviet political police—is an auxiliary structure (though sometimes a parallel structure, as it was during Stalin's Gulag era of 1936–1942) and has always been a party structure. The SS, although a party structure, under Himmler became independent of the Nazi party mostly because Hitler preferred the SS elite to his old Nazi cronies, the Alte Kämpfer and the Gauleiters. By 1942, the SS had become the most powerful instrument of the party, with the exception of the Führer himself. While the NKVD-KGB never became independent of the party-state, the SS did eventually become a semi-autonomous party and state instrument.

For most of the history of Chinese communism, the Chinese army shared power nearly equally with the party, and the parallel structures frequently clashed with the established bureaucracy or with auxiliary structures. Nevertheless, in the Chinese communist model, as in its bolshevik prototype, all sectors of society were politicized and coexisted with an exclusive public sector. In Franco's Spain and Salazar's Portugal, on the other hand, the dominant political structure was the dictator's cabinet; its composition changed infrequently, and its authority did not diminish as its members were replaced. Governments of Spain and Portugal, being oriented toward patrimonial and clientalistic patterns of authority, preferred not to support the unpredictable bureaucracies of parallel structures.

In modern military autocracies, the revolutionary command councils of the Middle East, Latin American military cabinets, Nasser's presidential office (1968–1971), and the national liberation councils of sub-Saharan Africa all parallel traditional executive structures. They hold the real power while the nominal executive is frequently demoted to the position of a technocratic cabinet. In several Arab praetorian regimes, real power is divided between the patrimonial and modern bureaucracies.

Some parallel structures may become auxiliary when they undertake mobilizational campaigns, as the Chinese Red Guards did between 1966 and 1971 during the Great Proletarian Cultural Revolution. Mutations of parallel structures are significant, for changes in their functions partially explain alterations in the regimes' orientation or, at least, the modification or revival of ideological stances.

After he assumed power, Hitler seemed to lose interest in the party; he never established a parallel party executive. Instead, he acted as a traditional despot and manipulated the party, the government bureaucracy, the military, and individual Nazis at will. Hitler had no desire to share power with the party. For him, the National Socialist party's last acts of mobilization were the election of 1932 and the putsch of 1934. After that, he abandoned the party to the mercy of the SS and rival political heirs—Goering, Goebbels, Himmler, and Bormann. While the Bolshevik autocrats in the Soviet Union and the senior Peoples Liberation Army (PLA) generals in China became the party and state apparatchiks, in Fascist Italy and Nazi Germany, the autocrats were transformed into führers and supreme leaders who resorted to traditional tyranny at the expense of the state, the party, and ultimately, of modernization of the economy.

Parallel and auxiliary structures, though analytically differentiated, are interchangeable and permeable; the distinction between them is neither clear nor consistent for all modern authoritarian systems. Auxiliary structures are sometimes autonomous political structures, sometimes project-oriented groups and sometimes voluntary associations designed to support the authoritarian regime. For instance, during the Cultural Revolution, the Red Guards were students, not functionaries. Similarly, women's, sport, hiking, mountaineering, family, youth, and traditional groups in Nazi Germany were harnessed to the party ideology and purposes. An auxiliary structure may not be institutionalized or organized and supported by the state; it could be a voluntaristic collective oriented toward enhancing state power. Such voluntary collectivities, whether vocational or functional, played a considerable role in Nazi Germany. Those in the USSR are directed and controlled by the party more firmly than were Nazi collectivities.

Auxiliary structures also represent the revolutionary and developmental aspect of the authoritarian state. They are formed, maintained, and recreated to eliminate old elites and shock into action new elites that have become victims of routine. The auxiliary structures represent the authoritarian regime's *élan vital* and task force. They embody its futuristic orientations, which sometimes border on the chimerical and which can be maintained only by revolutionary fathers like Lenin, Mao, Tito, Roehm, Himmler, and the Gang of Four. The auxiliary structure is also a political organization to regenerate and reform the stratified revolutionary movement. Thus, few auxiliary structures occur in praetorian or corporative systems; these are nonrevolutionary authoritarian states. The auxiliary structures principally maintain the regime's pristine spirit and are simultaneously instruments of political control.

The Seizure of Power: The Role of Auxiliary and Parallel Political Structures

Authoritarian regimes come to power during crises, most of them through violence. Those that do not assume complete control immediately (like the Nazis or some corporatists or praetorians) eventually seize power by force (*Machtergreifung*) or by emptying constitutional procedures of any real meaning. Revolutionary and coup-born political movements and groups often arrive in office with considerable preparation. In the Bolshevik, Nazi, and Fascist movements, the party's major purpose was to prepare for the seizure of power. The Nazi and Fascist parties were mobilized to seize power by parliamentary means and, as soon as they reached office, to destroy the liberal system. The Soviet model is the most conspicuous example of a political structure expressly designed for the seizure of power. Lenin, the professional revolutionary, believed that the party's chief function would be the seizure of power, and he scientifically established political structures and practices with this in mind. The agitprop machinery, the cadres, and above all, the auxiliary and parallel structures were designed for the seizure of power. Lenin's party-state is the model structure for both the seizure and maintenance of power.

The Nazis borrowed several ideas and structures from the Bolsheviks, especially the formation and manipulation of auxiliary and parallel structures, but they hardly intended to turn the Nazi party into cadre-and-agitprop-led copy. The nazi concept of the party was rather traditional. Its elements, like electoral mobilization and the role of support groups, duplicated those of contemporary social democratic parties or of other modern nonauthoritarian movements. Hitler (and Mussolini) did not establish single-party rule until after they had seized power, whereas Lenin's party was originally conceived for that role.

No corporatist group and few praetorian ones have created or adapted a party or movement solely for the seizure of power. Once in control, several such regimes have established single parties or coopted existing parties in hopes of institutionalizing rule, but none has succeeded in sustaining a party or movement effective enough to guarantee its rule.

For the Bolsheviks, parallel and auxiliary political structures were fundamental and permanent structures designed for the seizure of power; for the Nazis and Fascists, they were critical but temporary. But I would go further and argue that the degree, scope, and level of success of modern authoritarian systems depends on the institutionalization of the parallel and auxiliary structures. The more complex, adaptable, and flexible these structures are, the higher the authoritarian regime's level of stability and order. Certainly the failure of some modern authoritarian regimes (primarily corporatist and praetorian) depends not so much on their legitimation as on the efficiency and effectiveness of the instruments established for the *maintenance* of power. Because legitimacy must be invested in the political, as well as the ideological, instruments of control and of order, the classical political structures of liberal democracy or historical autocracy are inadequate for modern authoritarian rule and control.

The auxiliary and parallel structures, which Philip Selznick calls "the organizational weapon of communism," infiltrate social and political institutions and bring the turnabout when the appropriate time for political attack arrives. Although the Nazis and Fascists used auxiliary structures different from those of the Bolsheviks, their purposes for using these instruments, as in all modern authoritarian movements, were identical. Modern authoritarianism requires the political mobilization of social and electoral forces. The function of the auxiliary structure is to operationalize and fulfill the mobilizational, organizational, and ideological purposes of the authoritarian movement. Parallel structures function somewhat differently. They are designed to *legitimize* and help sustain the authority of the new regimes. Although they parallel such historical-classical liberal political structures as parties, parliaments, and cabinets, parallel structures do not resemble the classical legislative, executive, administrative, and judicial instruments. In the Bolshevik case the party is not exclusively engaged in electoral politics. The legislative bodies in an authoritarian system implement dictatorial, not electoral, demands. The judiciaries in authoritarian systems become subordinate to the ideology of the revolutionary or authoritarian movement.

Thus, the Supreme Soviet and other legislative and administrative bodies in the Bolshevik regime have purposes different from those of the historical-classical legislative bodies whose raison d'être is to represent individuals and interest groups. After 1926, the Nazi party became an electoral party with some auxiliary features (the political police, the propaganda machine, the youth and other elite guards) and it operated as such until after it had seized power and eliminated its most powerful auxiliary structure, the SA. In Fascist Italy, squadristi and the Fascist youth movement played a key auxiliary role in the march to Rome. Mussolini, like Hitler, first subscribed to liberal electoral and parliamentary political practices; however, he soon converted the Fascist party from an electoral party into an instrument for legitimizing fascism. In Germany, however, Hitler modeled his party after the mass Communist and Social Democratic movements, which were also liberal electoral parties. These and the Nazi party were engaged in an effort to capture the masses and established mini-auxiliary structures to penetrate the citizenry (youth movements and support groups). Electoral work was only one aspect of the parties' organization and purposes.

In corporatist authoritarian regimes, the corporatist structure is both auxiliary and parallel, replacing monarchical-conservative or liberal-socialist constitutional and parliamentary structures. Praetorians lack the structures needed for a takeover and usually are inadequately prepared for the seizure of power. As a result, they rely on military coups d'etat. Although they may try later to create a party sympathetic to the purposes of the army, the absence of effective structures of any sort (classical, auxiliary, or parallel), guarantees the permanent instability or illegitimacy of praetorian systems.

Modern authoritarian regimes are acutely concerned about their legitimacy, political survival, and sustenance. The elaborate and continuous use of parallel and auxiliary structures stems from this basic insecurity; the persistence of the party-state, the rise of the police state in Nazi Germany, and various control mechanisms in corporate and praetorian systems reflect it.

Authoritarian political systems are established, on the whole, in countries in which political conditions are unstable or deteriorating. Usually, authoritarian political systems are inherently weak and depend on buttressing by the police, use of terror tactics and support by political auxiliaries. (An exception is Castro's Cuba. Cuba's current regime is neither weak nor insecure and has not faced an internal threat since 1972. Cuba is unique because it does not use terror, except in isolated instances. As a result, it is not as vulnerable as other bolshevik regimes.) Parallel structures are installed to check the modern state's traditional political institutions: parties, parliaments, and the bureaucracy. They are supposed to safeguard the regime's control over society and to make sure that neither individual nor collective independent social action emerges. Like the regimes they replace, authoritarian systems are essentially weak and insecure, and most lack political legitimacy. Certainly, all modern authoritarian regimes are insurrectionary by nature, even if today's party-state has become conservative and antirevolutionary. Nevertheless, the cognitive and perceptive orientations of authoritarian rulers are deeply imbued with remembrance of things past, including brute force and insurrection, and therefore they continue to depend on auxiliary structures for control by terror.

Yet, the paranoid concern that stems from structural flaws, from the complexity of political institutions that are essentially captives of the parallel structures, and from the weaknesses inherent in a one-party or a nonparty state creates the seeds of the regime's destruction by obliging it to struggle to maintain the integrity of the one-party state, the machinery of terror, and the praetorian tyranny. Control, police and terror—instruments of the authoritarian political system—create a political momentum of their own: the fear of fear. The despot, the executive committee of the party-state, and the praetorian oligarchy are subject to double insecurity: fear of internal or external challenges and fear of their own instruments of terror. The Stalinist politics that reigned during the Yezhovshchina terror are an example of this insecurity. The Himmler terror machinery terrified almost every element of the Third Reich. The most significant aspect of Khrushchev's de-Stalinization policy was the destruction of Beria's terror system, the eventual taming of the political police, and the freeing of the party from the Stalinist yoke.

Thus, modern authoritarianism can best be understood as the *politics of permanent fear.* The system is not an impenetrable monolith dependent on permanent purges. Rather the protracted illegitimacy of a weak and vulnerable system feeds continuous political, structural, and personal insecurity.

Another significant political innovation made by modern authoritarianism is the almost totally bureaucratic state. Certainly, the party-state model could be described as a state bureaucratic system. In the absence of individual and collective social action and of a private domain outside the political system, bureaucracies perform *all* of the party-state's functions. As I shall demonstrate later, social and economic dynamics parallel organizational and bureaucratic dynamics. The Bolshevik model, however, is essentially a superpolitical organization, while the corporative and praetorian models approximate the administrative state.

The Nazi model was different from both. Germany had a highly developed state with a highly industrialized economy. Because Hitler essentially preserved the capitalist system, the Nazi state could not be characterized as bureaucratic or managerial. Even the party was not highly bureaucratized, although Himmler's police organization ultimately approximated a superbureaucratic structure. Preferring personal despotism and dependence on the political police and propaganda, Hitler deliberately preserved the capitalist system (which he needed to wage war) and neglected to bureaucratize society. He tamed the military and the bureaucracies only after Himmler had perfected his machinery.

Hitler's authoritarianism, although similar to the Bolshevik model in some respects, expressed itself more as a personal tyranny than through the total bureaucratization of society. In contrast, a party-state cannot survive if political structures and functions are not tamed and bureaucratized to the extent that the party permanently patrols society. Although the totalitarian school argues that the state must be bureaucratized in order to enable the regime to use terror and propaganda to control the society, these strategies could be used just as easily by a nonbureaucratic political system in which society has no defense against the instruments of terror. Paradoxically, in bureaucratized political systems—and the party-state is a superbureaucratic system—the machinery of control, the political structures of domination, and the auxiliary structures of terror cancel one another as often as they combine to brutalize the society as a whole.

The scope and level of the activity of parallel and auxiliary structures depend on the regime's degree of confidence in their role and on the absence of perceived opposition. In times of crisis established authoritarian structures or segments of them may become vehicles for the reinstitutionalization of authoritarian and despotic regimes. The politburo, the central committee, the military, the security section of the political police, the paramilitary structure of the regime, party, or state—all serve to ease the transition from one type of authoritarian rule to another (from party to police and back, from party to army and back, from the politburo to the central committee and back). Although the transition function is temporary, it is tremendously significant after the death of a despot (Lenin, Stalin, Mao); during oligarchical changes (Khrushchev to Brezhnev); in elite circulation (the years from Stalin's death to the present in the USSR, the period since Mao's death in China); during ideological revivals (the Cultural Revolution); and during wars (1941–1945 in the USSR, 1940–1945 in Nazi Germany and 1947–1949 in China). Of course, they play this role most importantly during serious challenges to the authoritarian oligarchy (1924–1927 in the USSR; 1953–1957 and 1976 in China, and 1933–1934 in Nazi Germany). The auxiliary institutions' ideological authority is at its height during these critical periods. The party temporarily defers to them and they come to "represent" revolutionary élan and purpose. The party, of course, quickly moves to reestablish its ideological primacy even when (as in the Cultural Revolution) revolutionary militants impugn its ideological purity.

When the modern authoritarian system is finally institutionalized, the auxiliary structures are either abolished, reduced in size and political influence, or integrated into the parallel structures. Once secure, the authoritarian regime no longer needs such parapolitical structures to crush opposition.

In summary, parallel and auxiliary structures represent the type of relationship between the authoritarian party and state and the orientations and aspirations of party and state elites. The latter decide when and for how long they are to employ their services. Usually, elites associated with auxiliary structures in revolutionary conditions (SA, Red Guards, the Gang of Four) are eliminated. Eventually, parallel and auxiliary structures become bureaucratic agencies of the party and the state.

Propaganda and Agitation

After the mobilizational party with its auxiliary and parallel structures, probably the most important innovation of modern authoritarian regimes is the machinery designed for agitation and propaganda. Harold Lasswell distinguishes agitation, "a method of collective influencing," from propaganda, which is "the technique

of influencing human action by the manipulation of repre-
sentations."[13] Propaganda is a system of symbol manipulation that
produces and leads to the acceptance of a collective ideology.[14]

The use of agitation indicates the transition from revolutionary
to institutionally mobilized authoritarianism. As Lasswell writes,
"In the agitational phase of social action, men are willing to die for
their convictions, and to forsake family and dependents in the service of the cause."[15] Agitation, or the organization of social energy
for social change, is one of the clearest manifestations of modern
mobilizational and revolutionary authoritarianism.[16]

Agitation and propaganda were probably major vehicles for the
formation, mobilization, and consolidation of bolshevism, fascism
and nazism. For Lenin, propaganda was an instrument to educate
the party.[17] Hitler used it to influence and mold the German
people. Both men used it in international politics as well. Lenin
sought to persuade other countries' "progressive elites" of the truth
and inevitability of Marxism, while Hitler's international propaganda was aimed at creating sympathy for a Germany "injured"
by the Versailles Treaty and at allaying fear of German military
might. Lenin used propaganda to advance social change; Hitler, to
further the cause of *Lebensraum* and Nazi imperialism.

Modern authoritarian regimes developed the machinery of agitation and propaganda highly. The Bolshevik (and Maoist) parties'
dedication to schooling apparatchiks, political leaders, and other
influential individuals in agitation and propaganda techniques
contributed fundamentally to their growth and sustenance. In this
respect, Hitler, Mussolini, and modern military autocrats lagged
far behind. According to Lenin, propaganda machinery should sustain the party by occupying a central role in training cadres. Since
propaganda plays a crucial part in fostering party cohesion in the
bolshevik state, it must be controlled exclusively by the party.[18]

13. *Encyclopedia of the Social Sciences* (1931) s.v. "Agitation."
14. *Encyclopedia of the Social Sciences* (1933) s.v. "Propaganda."
15. *Encyclopedia of the Social Sciences* (1931) s.v. "Agitation."
16. Ibid.
17. Alex Inkeles, *Public Opinion in Soviet Russia* (Cambridge, Mass.:
Harvard University Press, 1950), pp. 11–21.
18. Ibid., p. 43.

Hitler, on the other hand, used propaganda personally to project his image to the people and to institutionalize the concept of *Führerprinzip* ("principle of leadership"). Nazi propaganda, which was directed against Jews and "anti-Germans," simultaneously projected Hitler's image in an attempt to maximize the identification between the Führer and the people.[19] Military and corporate autocracies such as Spain and Portugal put much less emphasis on propaganda as part of the authoritarian machinery.

In Arab and sub-Saharan regimes and most praetorian states, parties do not exist; parties, if present, are at best auxiliary structures of the systems. They are not independent, as in the party-state, but fall into the category of parallel structures.

Authoritarian Control

Authoritarianism is a system of relationships between state and society and between political and societal sources of power. It is based on a type of domination which is dependent on centralized executive control and coercion. The type of authoritarianism is determined by the roles of the three political instruments of authoritarianism; the actual and relative political influence wielded by these political instruments; the preferential use of these instruments by the authoritarian regimes; the dynamics of authoritarian rule—for instance, which of the political instruments is used more effectively and when—and the relative influence in the long run of the political structures of modern authoritarian systems.

Authoritarianism is also a system that is designed to infiltrate the society and isolate it from the state, so that the latter has control over the former. Ideally, it is a system that makes a supreme effort to integrate the society into the mechanism of the state while giving the state ultimate control. "The executive in the authoritarian regime shapes and manipulates demands emanating from below while enjoying substantial leeway in the determination of

19. Ernest K. Bramsted, *Goebbels and National Socialist Propaganda, 1925–1945* (East Lansing, Mich.: Michigan State University Press, 1965), pp. 197–229.

the goals that the regime will pursue."[20] Authoritarianism does not necessarily result in efficiency, achievement of the common good, political integration, modernization, or order, even if most modern authoritarian regimes strive to achieve some or all of these goals. An ideal authoritarian system cannot tolerate cleavages, opposition, political pluralism, or even limited freedom of ideas. It does not deny constitutional authority, the rule of law and functional representation; however, these are modified by the absolute priority placed on order and stability.

Authoritarian systems pay considerable energy to the formation and development of political structures that control the executive, penetrate the society, and, above all, promote elite cohesion. These political structures deal with the problems of both individual and societal mobilization, modernization, and social change. The structures of authoritarianism—the single party, the propaganda machinery, the political police, the revolutionary command council, and the other corporate structures—all compete for the attention of the authoritarian ruler(s). These structures are the major consumers of the state's resources as well as the chief distributors of political and societal goods and services. They are also the sole source of elite recruitment for the authoritarian state.

The major purpose of modern authoritarian regimes is to establish the political elite's domination over society by arresting, subverting, or destroying autonomous individual, collective, and institutional behavior and thus to enhance the power of the authorities at the expense of autonomy. Social scientists interpret collective behavior to subsume different types of group behavior: collective excitement, social unrest, riots, mass hysteria, protest movements, primitive religious behavior, and reform and revolutionary movements.[21] Though the authoritarian regime will try to destroy disorderly and potentially antiauthoritarian forms of group behavior, it is dedicated to integrating other citizen and

20. Susan Kaufman Purcell, *The Mexican Profit-Sharing Decision* (Berkeley: University of California Press, 1975), p. 4.

21. Herbert Blumer, "Collective Behavior," in *A Dictionary of the Social Sciences*, ed. S. Gould and L. Kolb (Glencoe, Ill.: The Free Press, 1964), pp. 100–01.

interest groups, political parties, and social movements into the state. It does this by infiltrating and subverting these groups and inducing them to become part of the newly formed organizations aimed at political mobilization. The regime claims that it is establishing new forms of cultural behavior and is rearranging the social structure along so-called revolutionary and ideological lines. Briefly, authoritarian regimes attempt to coopt, subdue, or eliminate all sources of political power outside the state system, whether they are mass based or controlled by social elites.

Modern authoritarian states are distinguished from either classical autocracy or the liberal state by the combination of political elites and popular support and the political behavior this produces. The classical autocracy has no political elites and the masses have no political significance. In the liberal state, the political elites emerge from a competitive electoral process and independent social groups. To reiterate Schumpeter, they have been competitively chosen to make choices for the open electorate. In contrast, political elites in authoritarian states emerge mainly, if not exclusively, from the political structure. They are either state elites (from the bureaucracy and the military), party elites (ideological and functional), or parallel elites from the auxiliary or mobilizatory structures (youth, students, paramilitary, and political police).

The authoritarian political elites mobilize, support, or destroy competing social elites by using state and party instruments. They are not pluralistic since they are not chosen by an open, competitively oriented electorate. Their organization can take different forms—tyrannical, oligarchical, corporatist, factional, and coalitional. But what makes them significant is their linkage to the party-state (bolshevik, nazi) or to the state (fascist, praetorian, corporative).

Bolshevism, nazism, fascism, and praetorianism emerged from the collapse or weakness of regimes that suffered absence or severe crises of authority.[22] The success of authoritarian political elites

22. On the Fascist crisis of authority see Adrian Lyttleton, *The Seizure of Power: Fascism in Italy 1919–1939* (New York: Scribner's, 1972); Renzo De Felice *Interpretations of Fascism* (Cambridge, Mass.: Harvard University Press, 1977); and A. James Gregor, *The Fascist Persuasion in Radical Politics*, (Princeton: Princeton University Press, 1974).

depends, of course, on the types of regimes and elites they challenge and replace. Only monarchical or traditional regimes that collapsed because of wars as in Spain, Portugal, and Rumania, have become fascist, although fascist movements have emerged in other countries. Italy is an exception. Monarchical and conservative regimes rely on the crown, an established system, the aristocracy, and the military, which are all dedicated to the preservation of God and monarch. Modern authoritarian movements, on the other hand, are secular, nationalistic, radical, and republican.

The conservative establishment is linked to church, army, and aristocracy. The aristocracy is expendable in monarchical regimes, but the army is not. Such systems may spawn a new and even popular right, which advocates a form of radical nationalism.[23] The emergence of these rightist movements protects the monarch from destruction by the authoritarian regime although the two may come in conflict as in Franco's Spain and Antonescu's Rumania.

The rightist authoritarian regime faces a cruel dilemma because it cannot successfully replace conservative social forces and elites (this was true in Nazi Germany). Leftist radical authoritarianism (bolshevism) succeeded in eliminating the conservative, aristocratic social classes' political power and in establishing a monopoly over the state. Fascism, however, because it ended as a middle class revolution, never achieved a monopoly over the state. In authoritarian regimes of the left, the role of intellectuals and student movements is more prominent than in rightist regimes. In that respect, fascism should be placed on the left in the continuum of authoritarian movements and regimes. The intelligentsia, in the era before seizure of power, played a key role in the composition of both fascist and bolshevik elites.

All modern types of authoritarianism are highly bureaucratized. There is practically no recourse for those who seek independent political action and collective behavior. Control derives from almost total bureaucratization of the regime and of its in-

---

23. These ideas are taken from Juan J. Linz, "Conditions for and against Fascism in Interwar Europe" (Unpublished paper, Department of Sociology, Yale University, 1977).

struments of domination. The stress on policy diverts and reorients the traditional and historical political instruments into new types created by the authoritarian regime. The relative significance of the instruments of intervention and subversion determines the political structure likely to develop for domination and, therefore, the type of authoritarianism. Following this differentiation, I have established four fundamental modern authoritarian models: the party-state (Bolshevik Russia), the police state (Nazi Germany), the corporatist state, and the praetorian state.

Models and Political Structures of Modern Authoritarian Systems

All modern authoritarian systems are variations of these four basic models. Each model must be examined in terms of its institutions, because modern authoritarian systems have created new political structures and assigned new definitions, roles, and functions to existing institutions. Comprehending the strengths and weaknesses of these institutions and the dynamics of their relationships will considerably improve our understanding of authoritarian systems.

Evolution

The three major political components of modern authoritarian systems are the party, the constellation of parallel and auxiliary structures, and the state. The evolution of these three has always been idiosyncratic, shaped in all cases by the operation of two variables—the passage of time and the relative importance or influence of each component.

In the Soviet Union, for example, the party has been dominant from 1917 to the present, except when Stalinism was at its height and the despot, rather than the party, directed the secret police and the machinery of the gulags. Stalin purged the party of upper and middle elites from 1934 to 1938 and managed to annihilate its senior revolutionary elite. He also humiliated the state bureaucracy and purged 30 percent of the Red Army's officer class between 1937 and 1941. Nevertheless, the party withstood the challenge of

Beria and the secret police after Stalin's death and resumed supremacy. The party-state continues to this day.

In direct contrast, the National Socialist party, the major instrument of power in the nazi movement between 1920 and 1933, experienced continual fluctuations once Hitler attained power. The bureaucracy and the military, which Hitler had submerged during the early years of his rule, gradually grew stronger, especially from 1934 to 1938 and 1941 to 1943. During World War II, the military and the *Beamten* ("civil servants"), allied with the industrialists, posed a serious challenge to the authority of the party. An even more serious threat was posed by the secret police, which had been created as a party instrument in 1934. Ten years later, headed by Himmler, it had its own power base and the potential to threaten the führer's own power. During the war, the propaganda ministry under Joseph Goebbels was also certainly beyond state and party control.

Dietrich Orlow, the leading historian of the Nazi Party, is aware of the lack of consensus among authors on the relationship between the Nazi party and the Nazi state. "A question as basic as the relation of the party and the state under the Nazi system, surely one of the most fundamental problems of any totalitarian political society, is unclear.... The conclusions range from the affirmation that (unlike Stalinist Russia) the NSDAP was never able to challenge the priority of the state organs in the struggle for influence over German society to the exact opposite, with a compromise position offered by the statement that party and state engaged primarily in a process of mutual destruction."[24]

Although the SS was part of the Nazi party and included some of its most dedicated members, it was not cohesive but rather composed of several distinct factions. However, the function of a party in a party-state or in pluralistic systems is considerably different from that of the political police in authoritarian states. The SS, unlike the Soviet political police, was an autonomous group reporting directly to Hitler via Himmler, and Himmler was dedicated not to the advancement of the party, but to Hitler, to his personal

24. See Orlow, *The Nazi Party 1933–1945*, pp. 5–17.

interests and to the party's police function. Himmler and his SS, as well as the military SS (the Waffen SS), played a role in nazi politics independent from the party. It was crucial that Hitler support the independence of the SS when its rivals in the party criticized its role.[25] The party and its voluntary affiliates did continue to play a major role, however, in mobilizing the population during the war and in peacetime.

The party-state in Nazi Germany was not efficient. Although the party infiltrated the administration, it lacked the personnel to hold its own against the old, established bureaucracy. The SS, on the other hand, by acting as the führer's executive, was able to overcome the state administration and to act entirely independent of it. "It [the SS] became the real and essential instrument of the Führer's authority."[26]

In Italy, the Fascist party attained relatively strong influence only during the era of the *squadristi*. It can be argued that the decline of the squadristi, the party's official instruments, weakened the party's position. The corporatist structure established by Mussolini to resolve the problems of modernization and stability in Italy competed with the party and hastened the process of decay.

In both corporatist and praetorian states, the dictatorship—personal, oligarchical, or corporative—has dominated the bureaucracy and the police. In the praetorian system, party, police, and bureaucracy are all instruments of the military dictatorship, and the military, or the military party, is the sole autonomous political structure.

A modern authoritarian regime must create institutional political structures, whether openly or deceptively, actively or passively. These structures may include the following: a mobilizing party, a political police, a powerful military with coercive and interventionist capabilities, a chief executive with a loyal staff, a bureaucracy in the classical Weberian sense, and, above all, real or appar-

25. Although as Linz notes, the Nazi party was "resurrected" in 1944 (so were the SS and the Waffen SS), Hitler's purpose was to win the war not to revive the Nazi party.

26. Hans Bucheim, "The SS-Instrument of Domination," in *Anatomy of the SS State*, ed. Helmut Krausnick et al. (New York: Walker, 1968), pp. 139–40. Quote from p. 140.

ent instruments of mobilization, intervention and support. Whether these instruments actually work is conceptually a less important consideration than are the motivations behind their creation. No system, including a totalitarian one, works perfectly. The problems of these structures' capability, efficiency, and success therefore will not be considered here.

Locus of Power

The locus of political power in modern authoritarian systems can be identified by determining which political or functional structures provide recruits for the top political leadership.

The Party-state. Since 1917 the most important leaders in the USSR have been drawn from the party. Despite the country's modernization, the party has remained the source of recruitment for all functional elites, including the bureaucracy, the military, and the technocracy.[27] Thus the party (through the Central Committee) oversees the political and functional structures and the party coopts men by appealing to their desire for function and status.[28] Party dominance also extends to political structures at all levels from local to federal; this, combined with control of functional instruments, makes the USSR the prototypical party-state. (See figures 1.1 and 1.2.)

The party-state is best understood through examination of the role of the party's central committee. The central committee is the organ that buckles the state to the party; its secretariat and apparatus are immense, being designed to supervise governmental departments and agencies. It resembles state machinery and a real parliament and is the permanent reminder of the duality of the Soviet state. Relationships between the central committee and the state bureaucracy are complex and interlocking. The members or

27. For an analysis of political recruitment in the USSR, see Paul Cocks, ed., *The Dynamics of Soviet Politics* (Cambridge, Mass.: Harvard University Press, 1976).

28. On the role of the Central Committee as the reservoir of the Soviet power elite, see Robert Daniels, "The Central Committee of the USSR," in Cocks, *The Dynamics of Soviet Politics*, pp. 77–134.

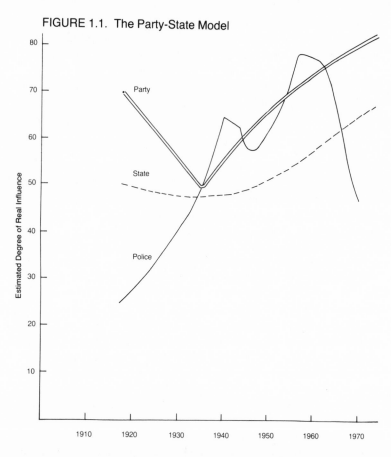

FIGURE 1.1. The Party-State Model

secretaries of the central committee are the power elite of the USSR. The Nazi party had had no such organization, nor super-governmental apparatus. Party leaders like Goebbels, Goering, and Himmler headed state ministries and agencies, but they were dominated by Hitler. Not unlike in nonauthoritarian systems, Nazi leaders served as Hitler's unofficial cabinet; however, no official cabinet existed in Nazi Germany. The USSR has a powerful cabinet—the Politburo. In Germany, the nazification of governmental agencies and departments was protracted and not the same in all departments—much depended on the personal style and aspira-

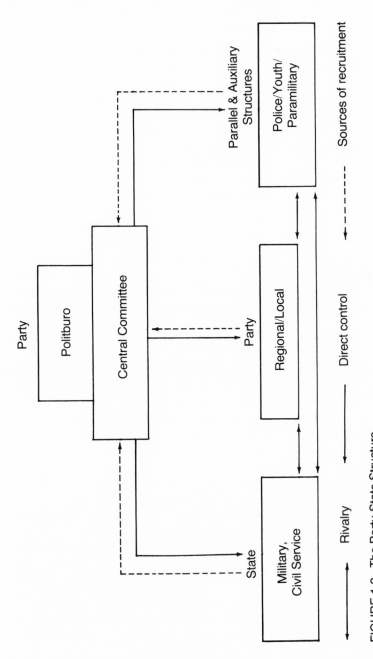

FIGURE 1.2. The Party-State Structure

tion of the particular Nazi leader. Goebbels, Himmler, Ley, and Ribbentrop were more active in nazifying their departments and agencies. In the USSR the Central Committee tightly supervises the departments and agencies of state that need not be bolshevized or communized. The Nazi leaders, having had no such central committee, preferred nazification to supervision of their departments.

The Soviet Central Committee Secretariat is involved in legislation, verification of party and government decision, auditing, policy making, and conducting investigations. No such functions and responsibilities existed in the Nazi party apparatus. It had no central committee structured like a minigovernment and no politburo to act as a cabinet. The Nazi government was never a party organ; the politburo is strictly a party organ. Yet both Stalin and Hitler made little use of their cabinets. For them the system of domination was strictly personalist; their cabinets were composed of their closest lieutenants. Professional and technical skills and proficiency were secondary to loyalty as the dictators' requirement of ability in their assistants. The Soviet Politburo has become more professionalized since Stalin.

The secretary general is not a professional bureaucrat; he is a professional politician. He is not primus inter pares; he has no equals, and this has been true of all of Stalin's successors. Collective leadership stops at the secretary general's desk; he is the most authoritative person in the USSR. A collective cabinet doesn't mean equal influence within the cabinet.

The Police State. The Soviet Union has been labeled as a police state by a wide variety of observers—Aleksandr Solzhenitsyn, Robert Conquest, and Richard Pipes, to name a few of the more prominent.[29] Pipes even awards the same label to czarist Russia. Viewed metaphysically, such atrocities as Stalinist brutalities, the horrors of Yezhovshchina, and the great purges all point to what could be called police state. For our purposes, however, neither

29. Pipes, *Russia: The Old Regime;* Robert Conquest, *The Great Terror,* 2d ed. (London: Penguin, 1970); and Aleksandr I. Solzhenitsyn, *The Gulag Archipelago 1918–1956,* 3 vols. (New York: Harper and Row, 1974, 1975, 1976).

philosophical impressions nor a narrow analysis of the role of the
political police is helpful. Instead, one must consider the relationship between the party and the police in the modern authoritarian
state. Viewed in this light, Nazi Germany, not the USSR, best approximates the ideal of a police state.

After the Nazi party gained supremacy in the 1929–1933 period,
it began to lose its zeal and passion for mobilization. By contrast,
the police, who originally had acted as the party's praetorian guard
and as Hitler's personal bodyguard, steadily amassed power. By
1944, the political and conventional police had been combined
under the sole direction of Heinrich Himmler.[30] Himmler's brutality and methodical leadership brought the police to a position of
autonomy and unparalleled ascendancy. His ambition clearly was
to become Hitler's heir apparent, and by the closing years of the
war his influence over the party, the military, and the *Beamten* was
an established fact. Lacking any viable competitor, Himmler was
within a hair's breadth of achieving Hitler's ultimate power because he controlled the police. (See figures 1.3 and 1.4.)

In the meantime, the führer continually reduced the party's
power, sometimes inadvertently and sometimes out of pure malice.
The party executive lost control over the *Gauleiter* (district leaders), who then engaged in internecine warfare; moreover, state and
local authorities were at the mercy of the political rivalry between
Gauleiters and *Beamten*. In this context, the institutional autonomy
of the SS allowed it to achieve equal standing with the party.
Hitler's elimination of the populist and revolutionary SA (storm
troops) with the help of the SS eventually opened the way to SS
dominance. The demise of the SA also momentarily strengthened
the military's autonomy, until the Fritsch-Blomberg affair in 1938
ensured SS ascendancy.

Responsibility for the initiation, conduct, and administration of
the final solution to the Jewish question also enhanced SS influence. Eventually it even possessed a fighting force—the *Waffen* SS.
In one decade the party and the police almost reversed roles, making Nazi Germany the only true police state so far.

30. The best and most reliable detailed study of the SS in Krausnick et
al., eds., *Anatomy of the SS State.*

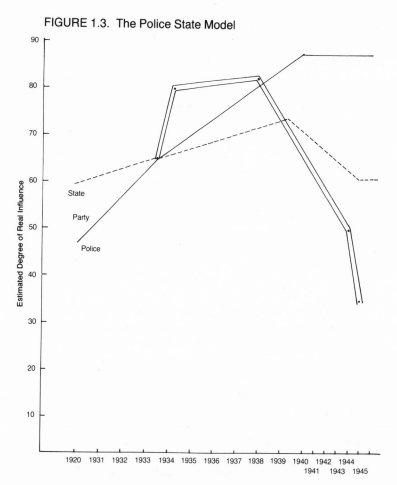

FIGURE 1.3. The Police State Model

Top political leadership during the short Nazi reign, however, came from neither the SS nor the state. Because most leadership had been established before 1934 by party members in their late thirties, party men and the SS continued to hold most of the important posts until the destruction of the Nazi state. Had the Third Reich survived, it is quite possible that the police would have begun to provide more and more leaders and that internal party rivalry between "moderates" and Himmlerites would have been considerable. Such a shift from party to police conceivably could have been reversed.

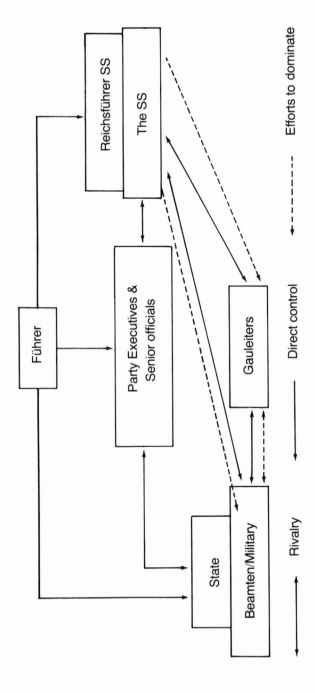

FIGURE 1.4. The Police State Structure

Führer

Reichsführer SS

The SS

Party Executives & Senior officials

Gauleiters

State

Beamten/Military

Efforts to dominate

Direct control

Rivalry

The Corporatist State. The corporatist state, which is usually oligarchical in nature, is dominated by a coalition of conservative or reformist politicians, the military, technocrats, and bureaucrats. Its most conspicuous political feature is the absence of an autonomous or powerful party. At most, the party is merely an instrument of the despot or the corporatist oligarchy. The rivalry between the state, the technocracy and the military is purely functional; the despot, even though his rule may be ephemeral, is in complete control, as Salazar and Franco have demonstrated.

Corporatist theory and ideology in Portugal during the period 1931–1975 was based on a statist and bureaucratic design intended to further modernization and maintain stability. Representatives to the corporatist chamber were chosen by the major functional and corporate interests (agriculture, commerce, industry) as well as by historical and classical corporate institutions (the military, the church, and such nuclear organic groups as the family and the local regional federations).[31]

To substitute for mobilizing organizations developed by the Nazis, Bolsheviks and Fascists, the corporatists evolved guilds (*gremios*).[32] In these associations the relationships between workers and employers and between landlords and peasants were of patron and client. Mobilization was also hierarchical, patrimonial, and clientalistic. Although the economic-functional "corporations" are the capstone of the entire system (see figures 1.5 and 1.6.) the most powerful structures are the military, the bureaucracy, and the church.

In Latin American corporatist regimes, the corporatist system, purportedly the supreme political structure of the state, is actually an inefficient and noninstitutionalized system of unequal and hierarchical relationships between autonomous and nonautonomous corporatist groups. The state dominates only with the active support of the autonomous corporatist groups: the military, the

31. These ideas are taken from Howard Wiarda, *Corporatism and Development: The Portuguese Experiment* (Amherst: University of Massachusetts Press, 1977), pp. 55–127.
32. Ibid., pp. 110–12.

FIGURE 1.5. The Corporate State Model

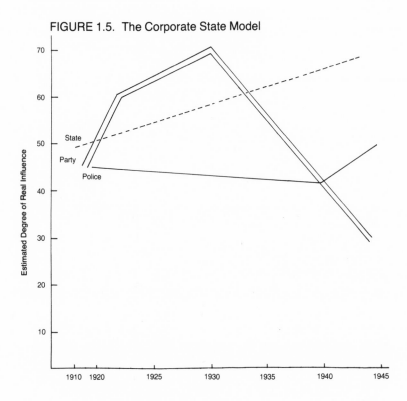

technocrats, and the church. The populist political party is one of
the weakest nonautonomous corporatist groups, which include the
economic-functional groups. The police is an instrument of both
the state and the military.

The Praetorian State. The praetorian state, or military dictatorship,
takes three forms: personal, oligarchical, and corporatist. The military dictatorship is often buttressed by an auxiliary structure, a
military party, whose major sources of support and recruitment
are the military, state bureaucrats, and technocrats. The executive
instruments that legitimize the regime's rule and exercise political
control include the military cabinet in some Latin American coun-

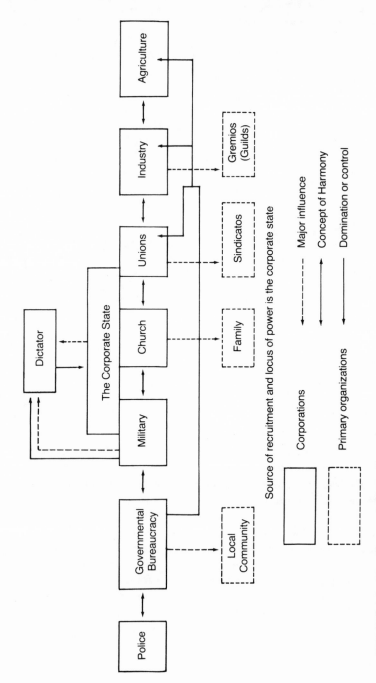

Source of recruitment and locus of power is the corporate state

Major influence - - - - - - - -

Concept of Harmony ↕

Domination or control —→

Corporations ▭

Primary organizations ▯

FIGURE 1.6. The Corporate State Structure

tries, the revolutionary command council in Arab military states, and the national liberation council in sub-Saharan Africa. These instruments are unique to modern praetorian states. In Latin America the military shares its rule with technocrats, industrial managers, bureaucrats, and the right-wing or reformist intelligentsia. But some Latin American military regimes (Chile and Peru, for example) do not engage political parties for support. In the Arab states, on the whole, the civilian members of the cabinet are not equal to the military members; and in some parts of sub-Saharan Africa, the military despot rules almost singlehandedly.

The praetorian state draws its major support from the military establishment though the military may not interfere in administration of the state, the economy, the police, and the military party. Arab praetorians typically either create a military party or harness an established nationalist or radical party. In Latin America, the praetorians may tolerate a populist political party (either leftist or rightist), although they retain the right to move from the barracks to the presidential palace if the party fails to comply with their demands. The military is obviously the locus of power in the praetorian state, even if only a few officers are visible. As in the corporatist state, recruitment is mixed, drawing from the bureaucratic, technocratic, and functional groups. Praetorian regimes take three subforms: personalist, oligarchic, and corporate.

The personalist praetorian model is a despotic tyranny (Amin's Uganda, Bokassa's Central African Empire, Mobutu's Zaire) or a despotic patrimony (Somoza's Nicaragua, Trujillo's Dominican Republic, Duvalier's Haiti). The system depends heavily on graft and sycophants; it is actually a kleptocracy (government by the ripoff artist), totally dominated by the despot.[33] The tyrant arbitrarily favors loyal regiments but does not control all of the military. (See figure 1.7.)

In Central America, the patrimonial despot typically establishes a constabulary system to sustain his oppressive regime. The Nicaraguan National Guard, for example, was trained by the U.S.

33. The term, not necessarily the concept, is taken from Stanislav Andreski, *The African Predicament* (London: Michael Joseph, 1968), pp. 110–33. See also Amos Perlmutter, "A Comparative Analysis of Military Regimes," *World Politics* 32, no. 1 (October 1980): 96–120.

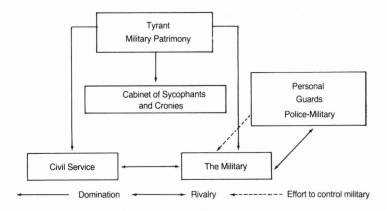

FIGURE 1.7. The Praetorian Tyranny: The Kleptocracy

Marines as an elite corps. Its original function was to protect the
Somoza family through a combination of military and constabulary functions. In sub-Saharan Africa, personal loyalty is a major
requirement of the national guard's officer clan.[34]

The oligarchic praetorian model differs from the personalist in
only one respect—in the oligarchic system, the military is autonomous. In Egypt, Syria, Iraq, Peru, and Ecuador, for example, the
military is always in a position to overthrow the military oligarchs,
who depend on the military establishment for support. The single
party or its surrogate institution are purely instruments of the
oligarchy (see figure 1.8.)

In the corporate praetorian model two structural forms, corporatism and clientalism, converge. The government is the most
powerful patron. Composed of military and technocratic groups, it
dominates the corporatist social system. The military, the church,
and the governmental ministries with their bureaucrats and
technocrats are autonomous corporatist groups, while the
functional-economic corporations are not. The corporations are internally and externally clientalistic and depend on the autonomous

34. See Richard Millet, *Guardians of the Dynasty* (Maryknoll, N.Y.:
Orbis Books, 1977), pp. 251–61.

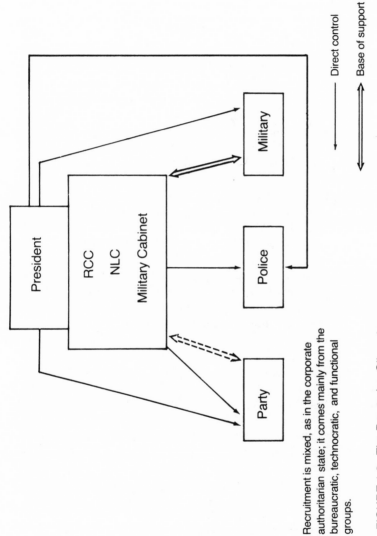

Recruitment is mixed, as in the corporate authoritarian state; it comes mainly from the bureaucratic, technocratic, and functional groups.

FIGURE 1.8. The Praetorian Oligarchy

groups. Although the military, the church, and the technocrats
serve as the regime's main source of support, the military is the
most powerful, acting as the arbitrator of the corporatist system.
(See figure 1.9.)

Time Sequence

Models seek simplicity and are often static; politics is dynamic.
The above models could be made more useful by adding the time
dimension. The Soviet model today scarcely resembles that of the
1920s. Increased economic, social and political complexity; the
war, Stalinism, and Khrushchevism; and the modernization,
specialization, and professionalization of functions in the USSR
necessitate modifications of the model, which nevertheless retains
its essential and heuristic value. Although the party is still the
locus of power, the distribution of power is more diffuse. The actions of the military, the economists, and the managerial classes as
well as the proliferation of functions have led to considerable
changes in the party-state structure. At the very least, the boundaries between party and state roles are now blurred and permeable, and within the party-state system the military and
managerial-technocratic groups have achieved semiautonomy.
Their scope of intervention, participation, and influence in both the
party and the state has broadened. The party's control over the
military, for instance, is no longer definitive.[35]

Janos describes the political processes of arbitration and the
noninstitutionalized restraints and the autonomous functions
exercised by the party-state of Eastern Europe.[36] There, the
Stalinist model has been surpassed by the autonomous "liberal"
modernization model, which strenghtened functional and professional elites and groups. In Yugoslavia after 1966, for example, the
centralized party oligarchy was transformed into a kind of "multi-
storied polyarchy of particular and institutionalized regional and

35. On the military, see Timothy Colton, *Commissars, Commanders
and Civilian Authority* (Cambridge, Mass.: Harvard University Press, 1979).
36. Andrew C. Janos, ed., *Authoritarian Politics in Communist Europe*
(Berkeley: University of California, Institute of International Studies, 1976).

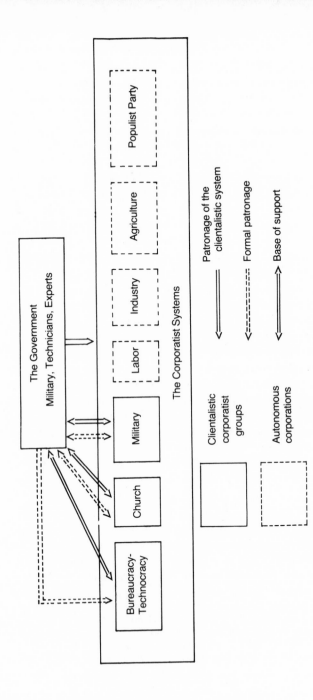

FIGURE 1.9. The Corporate Praetorian Model: Bureaucratic and Populist

functional interests."[37] Not only did four kinds of power centers emerge, but so did an impressive number of autonomously organized and institutionally legitimized forces as well as divergent interests.

In the Soviet model, changes in the distribution of power, resources, and influence between and within party and state considerably modified the former, more monolithic ideal. Yet all of these changes were still made within the framework of the party-state system. Incrementalism, rationalization of the economy, diffusion of ideology, and permeability between party and state did not change the fundamental model. To reiterate a point made by T. H. Rigby, the most salient characteristic of Soviet-type systems is their attempt to run all societal activities from a single center. The party continues to embody the organic aspects of the system, while the state bureaucracy is primarily responsible for routine performance. The mechanistic orientation, including the intricate pattern of roles, extensive bodies of procedural rules, and well articulated hierarchies of power and responsibilities, has superseded the organic model in both the party and the state. This development once more links the party to the state. Their dynamic adaptation, even if it now approximates the salient features of a complex and mechanistic organization, preserves the party-state duality.[38]

Time sequence also accounts for the various types of political struggles, coalitional arrangements, and political dynamics that are characteristic of stable authoritarian systems. In the USSR, China, Yugoslavia, and Czechoslovakia, the relationship between the party and the state is similar, even if their relative weight varies over time and with changing coalitional arrangements. Stalin used the party to annihilate the Leningrad party leadership allied with Zhdanov. Under Khrushchev the party was for the first time a conglomerate of factions in open rivalry. Mao attempted to use the Shanghai party group to destroy the central party leadership. When that strategy failed, he called on the support of the army and

37. Dennison Rusinow, *The Yugoslav Experiment: 1948–1974* (Berkeley: University of California Press, 1977), pp. 192–93. Quote from p. 346.
38. T. H. Rigby, "Politics in the Mono-organizational Society" in *Authoritarian Politics in Communist Europe*, ed. A. Janos, pp. 31–77. Quote from p. 45.

Lin Piao. The Czech Communist party was clearly divided between the pro- and anti-Dubček factions in 1968, a violation of the sacred Leninist dictum. This split would have destroyed the party-state monopoly had not Big Brother brutally annihilated the Dubček factions. According to Colton, the Soviet military could play a significant role in any serious party split. In post-Tito Yugoslavia, the party is divided into four factions, each backed by shifting coalitions of individual and group interests and ideologies: the republican and the provincial party-state apparatuses, the "managerial-technocratic" elites in the national economy, and the broad-based proletarian elite in the national economy.[39] Events in Poland following the rise of Solidarity in 1980 represent a challenge to the party-state by this alliance (not officially a party) of workers, peasants, and intellectuals. Here once more the party-state, Polish or Soviet, will not tolerate a serious challenge.[40]

The Yugoslav "separate road" and the other cases cited demonstrate that, despite the decay of ideology and the rise of communist polycentrism, the party-state duumvirate is the operative ideal and working basis for the Communist model in all of its forms. The breakdown of the party or the creation of a rival, even a communist rival, would end the party-state principle. Not only has this never occurred, but two countries—Cuba and Vietnam—have been added to the party-state system.

Another characteristic of the dynamics of authoritarianism is the shifting dominance of groups—party to police and back—as well as strife among party coalitions. Fascism and the Fascist party in Italy, for example, went through several transformations as the state progressed from syndicalism to corporatism between 1920 and 1943. Praetorian regimes in Latin America have shifted from oligarchic to corporate regimes and back again. In the Middle East, which is dominated by oligarchic praetorianism, shifts from corporate regimes to praetorian ones and vice versa are not unusual.

The party-state is distinguished from the corporative and praetorian types by its higher degree of elite stability and societal

39. Rusinow, *The Yugoslav Experiment*, pp. 192–93.
40. The most comprehensive analysis of the antiparty revolution in Poland is found in "Poland from the Inside," part 1, *Survey* 24, no. 4 (Autumn 1979), pp. 1–249; and part 2, *Survey* 25, no. 1 (Winter 1980), pp. 1–214.

conformity and by its institutionalized structure of authority. A central, hegemonic structure, a bona fide political elite and institutionalized authoritarian structures are lacking in the corporatist and praetorian regimes, to their disadvantage. Thus, the argument that party supremacy guarantees the totalitarian principle of ideological authoritarianism at all times is rather static. It is, in fact, a poor explanation of the complex phenomenon of modern authoritarianism.

Some authors are ready to extend analysis of political dynamics into the area of political culture. In Eastern Europe, for instance, they contend that an authoritarian political culture has prevailed from time immemorial, nurturing imperial, monarchical, conservative, fascist, and communist regimes alike. This interesting proposition contains too much cultural determinism for my taste: an iron law of authoritarianism, whether ancient and modern, is certainly suggestive, but not convincing. In Czechoslovakia, Poland, East Germany, and even Yugoslavia, the fate of the post-1945 regimes was not predetermined. Without Soviet guns, the KGB, and Soviet-assisted reinstatement of the exiled communist elite, I doubt that Czechoslovakia, Poland, and East Germany, especially, would have followed the supposed dictates of their political culture. As changes in Cuba, Chile, and Uruguay demonstrate, even corporatist political culture is not as resilient as suggested. In any case, an exploration into the linkages between political culture and my analysis of the role of authoritarian political structures is bound to be unfruitful. The political structures of modern authoritarianism are *modern* and *popular*, two characteristics that can hardly be related to political culture of premodern authoritarianism.

On the Limits of the Concept and the Models

A macropolitical analysis of generalizations from a selective review of history and politics is certainly made at the expense of micropolitical accuracy. Yet, in my view, comparable explorations in the social sciences and in history—often made at the expense of the latter—do not misrepresent historical and political facts even though they may oversimplify complex phenomena or fail to pro-

vide adequate explanations of events for which empirical information is meager. Some readers of this study would argue that my
model should not go beyond the three types of authoritarianism
that are obviously comparable, namely communism, nazism, and
fascism; that the explanation of political authoritarianism would
be overextended to include corporatism and praetorianism; and
that this study depends on an institutional explanation when no
universal normative acceptance of such a concept exists. Yet I am
convinced that the explanation of the political structures of
modern phenomena requires that corporatism and praetorianism
be included. Unquestionably, institutionalized authoritarianism
(communism, nazism, and fascism) represents a higher and more
complex relationship between state and society as well as a much
higher degree of elite cohesion. In corporatist and praetorian regimes, a much looser relationship prevails between the state, the
party, and the bureaucracy. It can also be argued that state and
party do not have the same epistemological meaning in communist
and in praetorian political systems. Praetorian and corporatist regimes are not cohesive, integrated, or systemic; above all, they are
not authoritative. Neither were the historical and classical autocracies nor, possibly, praetorian tyrannies. Yet it is not the command economy, the collectivist ideology, or the integration and
symbiosis between party and state and between bureaucracy and
military that are the motivating political forces and the institutional raison d'être of the political structures of modern authoritarianism. No system, not even that of the Soviet Union, East
Germany, or China, is monolithic. But no system lacks a motivating institutional-ideological purpose either, and the corporatist
and praetorian political structures are both *modern* and *authoritarian*. Their orientations are rational, in the Weberian sense, even if
their politics are patrimonial and personalist, their institutional
arrangements noncooperative, and their political structures nonin-
tegrated. They all subscribe to a similar model of political and institutional organization.

   Ideally, authoritarian political organizations are large in scale,
highly centralized, and bureaucratized. All these regimes share a
similar organizational ideology: they aspire to become modern by
securing the political support of the many (who are then manipu-

lated by the few) and to become authoritarian through centralization. This ideology not only explains the political motivation of
their makers and rulers but also brings the corporatist and praetorian cases into the model of authoritarianism offered here. The
realities are, of course, quite different. Corporative political structures are not successfully centralized; they are inefficient, fac-
tionalized, noninstitutionalized, and unstable. And praetorian systems have no party or parties worthy of the name. In such systems,
the state is weak because it is governed by elites that are neither
cohesive nor politically integrated. Nevertheless, all of these systems are oriented toward large, highly centralized, and bureaucratized structures.

Obviously the limits of my model depend on the scope and level
of relationships between the various authoritarian political structures. What this model offers is a *relative* and *relational* explanation
of the behavior of one genre which I call modern and authoritarian.
All of the political structures of modern authoritarianism—the
party, the state bureaucracy, the military, and the political
police—strive to establish large-scale, centralized, bureaucratic
control. They are collectively the motor of the authoritarian system. The rational (in the Weberian sense) authoritarian model also
can be achieved by traditional patrimonial means, orientations,
and political relationships. The explanation for modern authoritarian behavior must be dynamic, not static as the totalitarian
school's model is. Only an emphasis on dynamic relationships can
explain why the ineffective, nonparty system in Egypt under Nasser and Sadat is of the same genre as both Brazil's corporate regime and the Lenin-Mao party-state system. Such an approach analytically yields a better understanding of the political dynamics of
the above phenomena than does treating the corporatist-
praetorian and the communist-fascist systems separately.

Certainly the competitive, noncentralized, and pluralistic
model based on the ideas of John Locke and Adam Smith cannot
explain the political behavior of corporatist-praetorian systems.
The model I propose yields better explanations for the behavior of noninstitutionalized authoritarian political structures because it locates all political structures that share an orientation
toward centralized and hierarchical organizations on the same
continuum. This is precisely why, for me, this pioneer effort has

yielded so much. It sheds a new light on modern phenomena: the political structures of authoritarianism. These political facilities, whether efficient or inefficient, are invented or adopted by modern systems. The cohesion and sustenance of grand, hierarchical, and centralized organizations in corporatist, praetorian, and even fascist political systems are important subjects for analysis in another treatise.

The Military and the Authoritarian State

In both institutionalized and noninstitutionalized regimes, the modern authoritarian state is linked to a large-scale military organization. The special relationship between the party and the army in highly institutionalized authoritarian regimes is of particular interest.

In Nazi Germany, Hitler did not depend on the political support of the military. He subordinated these political simpletons to the Nazi party and frequently purged the army,[41] even though very early in the regime the military's support, along with that of the conservatives, was crucial to Nazi success.[42] Stalin also subordinated the military. Yet Timothy Colton argues that the Soviet military's coercive capability allows it to seize power in a way "not fundamentally different from that followed by soldiers in other societies,"[43] by which he means that it wields considerable influence. In addition, it is argued that the military's ideological capability is not limited by the party and the state—the twin instruments of authoritarianism in the USSR. The USSR's military, corporate, ideological, and institutional interests therefore could converge and even pressure the military into intervening in the political sphere. Thus the military in the USSR could play the same role the military did in China: regenerate pristine bolshevism, that is, Leninism.[44] Although these hypotheses seem intellectually exciting, they are politically implausible. Colton himself vigorously de-

41. Perlmutter, *The Military and Politics in Modern Times*, p. 57.
42. K. J. Muller, "The Army in the Third Reich: An Historical Interpretation," *Journal of Strategic Studies* 2, no. 2 (September 1979): 123–152.
43. See Colton, *Commissars, Commanders and Civilian Authority.*
44. Ibid., pp. 221–49.

fends the notion that the Soviet military has historically been politically quiescent.[45]

The party-state in the USSR, as in other authoritarian states
(including China and Nazi Germany, where any successor to Hitler
would have had to depend on the military's support as Hitler did in
1933–1934), unquestionably needs support from political groups
and structures. The military, as one of the most conspicuous, could
actively intervene, acting as a surrogate regime and as savior of the
party-state. It could also act as an ad hoc auxiliary structure to
regenerate bolshevism. But that sort of intervention would not
necessarily abolish the party-state. On the contrary, once bolshevism was rejuvenated, the military could well return to the
barracks—as parts of it did in contemporary China. In the USSR,
China, Vietnam, and Cuba, as in praetorian systems in which it
acts as arbiter, the military will "protect the constitution from the
barracks," to reiterate the Kemalist dictum.

Unlike the praetorian or corporatist regimes, the party-state
represents a network of complex organizations whose relationships
with each other are not neutral and isolated but integrated and, in
some cases, symbiotic. There are periods of intervention and relatively brief intervals of isolated neutrality. In the party-state, the
military is one of the regime's major allies even when the party
must establish its iron rule over the state and the society. Thus,
although the military praetorian can set itself up as the sole ruler
or as an arbiter among several factions within the regime, the
party-state military intervenes to protect the party from Bonapar-
tist elements among the institutional elites. In other words, usually
the military does not intervene against the party, but it will support one faction during an interelite struggle. For example, both
Khrushchev (1957), and Mao Tse-tung (1966–1967) successfully recruited military support as a political tactic. A similar process occurs in praetorian regimes when civilians recruit military men for
support of a coup.

In the Soviet Union, the army, whose institutional autonomy
has been growing since 1917, assumes four roles: protector of the
CPSU's waning legitimacy; guardian of the party's ideological-

45. Ibid., pp. 250–78.

revolutionary heritage; quasi-revolutionary agent of Soviet interests in the Third World; and traditional defender of the homeland. In the last twenty years, the party-army relationship in the USSR alternated between military dependency on the party and autonomy; the party and army have at times collaborated and at other times expanded at each other's expense. This was also true in Nazi Germany.

Civil-military relations in the Soviet Union are symbiotic. They are shaped by important systemic, structural, and ideological limits, such as the hegemonic power of the single party, the absence of a constitutional means of transferring power, security and paramilitary organizations within and outside of the military establishment, and the Marxist-Leninist tradition that views standing professional armies as antirevolutionary forces and threats to party hegemony.[46] More than other institutional structures in the USSR, the military has developed special institutional loyalties to and relationships with the party and the state. Its professional concept of responsibility and mission and its associative corporate values guarantee not only its political quiescence but also its partnership with the party. The party, in turn, enhances the military's political influence and privileged position.

In both China and Cuba, the symbiotic relationship between party and army is even stronger. In China, although professionalization since the 1950s has enhanced the military's autonomy, the military remains a major political actor in the 1980s. Between 1920 and 1980 China also experienced alternating dependency and autonomy between party and army. At times, the distinction between the two was practically nonexistent; other times, the military was relatively neutral. During the Cultural Revolution, the military leadership demonstrated the political importance of the intimate relationship between the two most powerful structures of Chinese communism. At first the military became Mao's mailed fist against the party leadership; later on it was used as the protecting shield of the party against Lin Piao and his cohorts. Without the army, the

46. Roman Kolkowicz, "The Future of Civil-Military Relations in Socialist Countries: The Soviet Union" (Paper delivered at Conference on Civil-Military Relations in Socialist and Modernizing Societies, **Santa Barbara**, Calif. May 17–19, 1979), p. 14.

party might have been further weakened and fragmented. Just as Mao used the army to bring about a return to pristine communism, his successors used it to restore order in both the party and the state.

Rather than withdraw at the end of Cultural Revolution, however, the military consolidated its political position and strengthened its domination of the regional power structures. Although this action coincided with the reconstruction of the party,[47] the military's limited disengagement from politics demonstrates that the upheaval is not completely over; the military still serves as the revolution's praetorian guard. The military will continue to play an important role in the politics of leadership succession in China, just as it does in the USSR. Teng Hsaio-ping and the party presently maintain the party-army relationship.

Withdrawal by the military in communist systems coincides with relative party stability; the eras of intervention are linked to political crisis. The most important crisis management and conflict resolution is accomplished within the party with the participation of both the army and the party.

Cuba also demonstrates the symbiotic and almost organic relationship between the army and the party.[48] The armed forces in Cuba, the Fuerzas Armadas Revolucionarias (FAR), began as the politico-military vanguard of the revolution in 1959 and gave birth to the Cuban Communist Party (PCC) in the early 1960s. If the Chinese Revolution was born in the bosom of the People's Liberation Army the Cuban Revolution is the progeny of the FAR. The FAR predates the PCC, and the latter's subordination to the military command was clearly reflected by tasks of the Party apparatus. As William LeoGrande notes: "The Party apparatus in the FAR was

47. I am grateful to Ellis Joffe for his incisive commentary. See Ellis Joffe, "The Military as a Political Actor in China" (Paper delivered at Conference on Civil-Military Relations in Socialist and Modernizing Societies, Santa Barbara, Calif., May 17–19, 1979), p. 20.
48. Here I have found the pioneer work of my colleague William LeoGrande enlightening. See his seminal pieces "The Politics of Revolutionary Development: Civil-Military Relations in Cuba, 1959–1976" *The Journal of Strategic Studies* 1, no. 3 (December 1978): 260–95; "The Case of Cuba" in *Civil-Military Relations in Communist Systems*, ed. Dale Herspring and Ivan Volgyes (Boulder, Col.: Westview Press, 1978), pp. 201–18.

organizationally integrated into the PCC through the Military Commission ... of the Central Committee of the Party."[49] The national PCC apparatus was too weak to dominate the FAR, but as the PCC developed, it was not subordinate to the FAR. Yet the FAR's influence in the PCC was substantial.

In the communist system, the military is Janus-faced. It is the guarantor of the civilian party regime and the protector of party hegemony; the latter role implies that it will intervene in party affairs during hegemonic crises. According to Kenneth Jowitt, in Rumania the relationship between party and army is alternately consensual and conflictual as both compete for heroic roles.[50] Ceauşescu, the party's leader, is the key figure: he resolves conflicts just as Lenin, Stalin, Mao, Ho Chi Minh, and Kim Il Sung did, generally at the expense of the military's institutional autonomy.

As surrogate for a maximum leader in the USSR, reconciliation of the party-army conflict has been routinized by the Politburo which is the system's arbiter. Thus in the USSR the relationship is complex. In the present era of collective leadership, the military certainly enjoys greater institutional autonomy than in the past, but that does not imply that a group conflict model provides a better explanation of post-Stalinist phenomena than do the political and bureaucratic models. The leader or collective leadership still represents the final arbiter of the contest for hegemony in the party-state. In Yugoslavia, the military never ceased to be part of Tito's party-state. Yet Tito's death creates the potential for a collective leadership to change the relationship between the party and the army. Nevertheless, such a leadership would probably reiterate the principle of partnership in order to protect the party-state during periods of cooperation and conflict.

Could authoritarian party-state regimes survive without the military? My answer is no. The military performs the essential function of protecting the party's hegemony even when that role conflicts with its own self-image and institutional autonomy.

49. LeoGrande, "Civil-Military Relations in Cuba," p. 209.
50. Kenneth Jowitt, "Heroic and Hegemonic Party-Military Relations in Eastern Europe: The Case of Romania," (Paper delivered at Conference on Civil-Military Relations in Socialist and Modernizing Societies, Santa Barbara, Calif., May 17–19, 1979).

Without the military, the reign of the party-state might come to an end.

Party-states, at least socialist ones, have always been more interested in policy results than in formal procedures. Thus the procedural "rules of the game" for resolving serious policy conflicts tend to be implicit, vague, and highly flexible. "Winning" within the party is usually (but not always, as Mao's experience showed) decisive, and victory generally is achieved "by any means necessary." The lack of reliance on procedure is derived from both ideology (Marx's theory of the state, for example) and the very existence of hegemony: no other center of power is sufficiently autonomous to challenge party legitimacy on procedural grounds. To the extent that the symbiotic party-army relationship exists, winning a policy conflict in the party is the same as total victory.

If the army could be removed or its neutrality guaranteed, a losing faction within the party might refuse to surrender. That is, it may carry the struggle into other arenas with no fear of military retribution as Mao did when he appealed to the masses at the outset of the Cultural Revolution. In such cases, the losers are unlikely to feel bound by the ephemeral procedural rules of inner-party debate and conflict resolution. As a result, they might take actions that would actually challenge the hegemony of the party and hence the very essence of the party-state. In sum, the military essentially restrains intraelite conflicts to within party bounds; challenges to party hegemony are more likely when the procedures for resolving intraparty conflict are poorly developed and often ignored. The absence of an institutionalized and autonomous military not only could magnify intraparty conflicts but could encourage systemic, structural, and ideological challenges to the party-state. Absence of the military poses an implicit threat to the party's revolutionary goals and an explicit threat to the party's coercive and mobilizational control in the form of generalized structural and societal conflict that the party itself could not contain. Consequently, the military's interventionist functions endanger the party substantially less than more serious political threats from all sides. As the historical experience of the USSR clearly demonstrates, even the military's weakness threatens the party. A weak, isolated and dependent military establishment leads to crises of authority, legitimacy, and security for the party. Unlike praetorian systems, in which the army is a serious and continual threat to authority, legitimacy, and order, the Soviet and the Chinese military contribute heavily to political and economic development and, above all, to maintaining the party's security and its commitments to foreign and defense policies. I agree with Kolkowicz that these relationships are not forged without conflict. The military is, also, well aware that its own existence is endangered if the party-state collapses.[51]

China and Cuba provide conspicuous examples of the primary role that the military plays in institutionalizing the party. In Cuba, the army was instrumental in the creation of the party; in China it led an effort to reform both the party and the state. The military is the link that binds the party to the state; without it single-party authoritarianism could not be sustained. Colton has described the army as a vehicle for participatory mobilization. The military's participation in politics is the normal and natural state of affairs in the party-state system. As guardian of the heroic party and its ideology, and as a potential coercive instrument, the army is political and politically oriented. Tolerance of military participation in Soviet, Chinese, Cuban, and Yugoslav politics is high, it being deemed of its own definition protection of the Communist Constitution and, consequently, of party supremacy. Theoretically, disappearance of the military in the party-state could push the regime from Communism toward praetorianism. The army therefore protects the regime from the praetorian syndrome prevalent in and characteristic of noninstitutionalized authoritarian regimes. As Colton properly points out in his study of the USSR: "a more appropriate approach is to orient the analysis toward military *participation* in politics rather than the process of civilian control over the military."[52] However, Colton assumes incorrectly that a high rate of military participation in the party-state places the regime in jeopardy. A conflictual relationship between the party and the army in a party-state is not the same as the absence of any viable

51. See Kolkowicz, "Future of Civil-Military Relations in Socialist Countries," pp. 14–17.
52. Colton, *Commissars, Commanders and Civilian Authority*, pp. 231–49.

relationship between a strong military establishment and a weak regime, which is characteristic of oligarchical praetorianism. Inequality of civilians with the military enhances praetorian regimes, except in states in which the party and the army are relatively institutionalized and autonomous (Syria and Iraq are prominent examples that will be discussed later).

The conflict between the party and the army in the party-state system enhances the political power of both institutions and the stability of the regime as a whole. The military's institutional and societal goals and values are congruent with the party's, even though their internal values may not converge. As Colton writes, "In comparative perspective, the Party-Army relationship has been remarkably free of direct conflict, and the safest prediction is that such confrontation will be avoided in the future."[53] Odom, in opposition to Kolkowicz and Colton, correctly identifies the consensual aspects of party-army relationships; their alignments are horizontal, and the military is not only an administrative arm of the party. Disputes over military policy do not follow civil-military lines but originate within party factions and over budgets.

According to Odom, Kolkowicz and Colton underestimate the extent of party-army interlocking. The party-army relationship has symbiotic aspects in domestic politics in that both share many values even if their roles are clearly differentiated; political values are not necessarily identical with political roles. In short, "the military [in the USSR] is first and foremost a political institution."[54] But, in the modern authoritarian system, the military is dependent on the central system—the party. In a civil war, the military "would reinvent the Party or one very similar."[55]

Some would argue that the tight relationships between the army and the party could disintegrate. I would argue, however, that this kind of fragmentation could not occur in an institutionalized, authoritarian political system. In fact, in any institutionalized authoritarian system (that is, a party-state sys-

53. Ibid., p. 232.
54. William I. Odom, "The Party-Military Connection: A Critique" in *Civil-Military Relations in Communist Countries*, ed. Dale Herspring and Ivan Volgyes (Boulder, Col: Westview Press, 1978), pp. 25–52.
55. Ibid., p. 43.

tem), the military forces the party to unify itself during periods of stress and conflict. In the modern authoritarian state, the military is a central political and bureaucratic structure, sometimes endowed with considerable executive power. The most interesting political development of the party-state system is that the linkage between two competing structures also promotes political stability because it modifies the excesses of both. No democratic political system would and no praetorian system could tolerate this type of relationship between the central instrument of political control and the military establishment.

The Cuban model offers an intermediate case between the communist and noncommunist civil-military relationships. The composition, structure, and orientation of the Cuban army-party regime is derived from a symbiosis between military and political party elites. The Cuban military is neither a strategic elite; an alliance of the military, civil servants, and assorted politicians; nor a role-expanding institution. In Cuba the military may create the single party or the single party may be the military's vehicle of rule and authority. This special relationship is of particular interest because, unlike the three types previously discussed, the army-party regime represents a network of relationships between complex organizations.

Although critics question whether Castro's Cuba is a military regime, I believe it has been a military regime of the army-party type since 1971. Before that the military alone was the single most authoritarian elite. In Cuba, at the present time, the party and army relationships are integrated and symbiotic.

The military in an army-party regime is always one of the regime's major allies. The link is not between civilian and military elites but between two separate and relatively powerful political organizations: the party and the army. The military is the protector of the party, guarding its legitimacy and pristine values. The military also acts as a quasi-revolutionary agent and the guardian of the ideological heritage, playing a key role in the transfer of power and ensuring national security. Both the party and the army tolerate a high degree of penetration by the other. Because of the tight links between the two organizations, military intervention in politics is both natural and constitutional. The military functions as a political party, an instrument for interest articulation, and an avenue for elite political mobility. The bond between the military and the party is exemplified by relations among Cuba's leaders. As LeoGrande points out:

> Cuba has been ruled in large part by military men who govern large segments of both military and civilian life, who are the bearers of the revolutionary tradition and ideology, who have politicized themselves by absorbing the norms and organization of the Communist party, and who educated themselves to become professional in politics, economics, managerial engineering, and educational as well as military affairs. Their civilian and their military lives are fused.[56]

The military in the army-party regime is both a parallel and an auxiliary political structure. To buttress the authoritarian and revolutionary regime and to facilitate mobilization, the military in Cuba (and in China and communist Vietnam) either creates, or itself becomes, a parallel political structure. The military and the party are parallel in the sense that both duplicate the traditional functions of political institutions. The army becomes a party, a legislative body, and the protector of revolutionary values. These military-political structures are also the armed instruments of political takeover, and they defend the party against corruption and "decadence." The military works with the party in organizing and controlling propaganda, cultural activities, economic modernization, professional groups, and, of course, national security.

The Cuban experiment is analogous to the Soviet dual state, but in Cuba the military has greater autonomy and a more important political role. During the 1960s the predominance of the Cuban rebel army, which, for example, carried out the agrarian and land expropriation, gave it a central role even after the party's creation. Throughout the 1960s, the party apparatus that was part of the military was the most developed section of the party and had tremendous influence in the party as a whole. The party and the army's authoritarian, professional, and revolutionary norms; organizational skills; and elites were intertwined. The military command

56. LeoGrande, "The Politics of Revolutionary Development," p. 289.

and the party's revolutionary functions were autonomous but politically integrated. But, as LeoGrande correctly observes, in a comparative perspective the Cuban experiment "suggests the potential applicability of two different models of civil-military relations." The first is a model of civil-military relations in underdeveloped nations; the second, a model of civil-military relations in communist political systems.

The symbiotic relationship between the Ba'ath party and the Syrian and Iraqi militaries is reminiscent of the Cuban case. In both Iraq and Syria there is an analogous mutual dependency and organizational autonomy of party and army. Similarly, the relative stability of the Syrian and Iraqi Ba'ath regimes should be linked to the dual party-army governance. This symbiotic relationship is demonstrated by the fact that the Syrian army protects the élan of the neo-Ba'ath in Syria just as the party inculcates élan into the Iraqi army. Yet the analogy ends here. Neither Syria nor Iraq progressed through the revolutionary and mobilizational stages Cuba did. Instead, the Syrian and Iraqi army-party relationships strengthened the army-party elites and enhanced their political mobility. In neither country did the revolution go very far; both are examples of army-party regimes that are not very highly institutionalized. In Syria the Ba'ath, the presidency and the military are relatively autonomous political institutions. Although the president is clearly the most powerful, he could not govern effectively without the party and the army. The latter are parallel structures that have political influence and are sources for elite recruitment.

Despite these differences, the Syrian and Iraqi regimes are guaranteed greater stability than are tyrannical and oligarchic praetorian regimes. The installation of the new elites and the creation of a relatively effective Syrian state that dominates society and the military was a product of a party-army symbiosis. Both the elaborate military organization and the Ba'ath created a new kind of military regime in the Middle East. Organizational autonomy and symbiotic relationships between the party and the army enhance stability in the case of Iraq, Syria, and Cuba.

Clearly a relationship between the central state and the large-scale political organization characterized by oligopolistic competition among civilian and military elites for domination of the hegemonic political structures is a feature of the political dynamics of *all* modern authoritarian states, whether stable or unstable, institutionalized or praetorian. The military has a central role in the modern authoritarian state—in the USSR and China, Brazil and Egypt, Cuba and Rumania, Syria and Peru, just as in Nazi Germany. The symbiotic, conflictual, and cooperative relationship between civilian and military elites clearly typifies the era of the central state, the grand organization, the hegemonic party, the interventionist military, all of which operate at the expense of the society, the individual, and genuine political pluralism.

Totalitarianism and Authoritarianism

The place of ideology in authoritarian regimes is exceedingly controversial.[57] At the risk of being challenged by the totalitarian school, I assert that while ideology plays a substantial role in the development of bolshevik and nazi authoritarianism, it plays an insignificant part in the evolution of military and corporate praetorian autocracies. The totalitarian school argues that ideology (messianic, racist, anti-Semitic) is an organic, and the most conspicuous, component of mass authoritarianism. It may be successfully demonstrated that the three most notorious authoritarian ideological movements in modern times—bolshevism, fascism, and nazism—were the primary or necessary political vehicles for the establishment of the authoritarian regimes that supported them. Certainly the party-ideology nexus was fundamental to the totalitarian structure of these movements. Nevertheless, I will argue that an examination of political structures is the most useful tool

57. The literature on totalitarianism is extensive. The classical definition and explanation are found in Hannah Arendt, *The Origins of Totalitarianism*, new ed. (New York: Harcourt Brace, 1966); Carl J. Friedrich, *Totalitarianism* (Cambridge, Mass.: Harvard University Press, 1954); Jacob L. Talmon, *The Rise of Totalitarian Democracy* (Boston: The Beacon Press, 1952); C. J. Friedrich and Z. K. Brzezinski, *Totalitarian Dictatorship and Autocracy* (Cambridge, Mass.: Harvard University Press, 1956); and Zbigniew Brzezinski, *The Permanent Purge* (Cambridge, Mass.: Harvard University Press, 1955).

to explain the political behavior, structural arrangements, or political dynamics of modern authoritarian regimes.

Since the principal object here is to analyze the dependent variables of modern authoritarianism, I find the totalitarian school's explanation of little use. In a study of authoritarian political behavior, Arendt's existential thesis that totalitarianism is an effort to change the nature of man and the nature of nature is not very useful. Neither is Talmon's concept of the utopian aspirations of the Enlightenment's totalitarian democrats to fulfill the rational postulates of the French Revolution by realizing the "sole and exclusive truth in politics." Talmon's metaphysical concept of political messianism is not a viable tool for the political scientist seeking to understand the nature of the modern "totalitarian democracy" (bolshevik, nazi, or fascist) any more than is Brzezinski's concept of the "permanent purge" for explaining Soviet politics from Lenin to Brezhnev.

Furthermore, Talmon's distinction between the totalitarianism of the left and of the right does not help to differentiate between bolshevism (presumably leftist totalitarianism) and nazism (rightist totalitarianism).[58] It is equally impotent in explaining either the party's domination of the state in the USSR or the domination by Hitler and his political police of both party and state in Nazi Germany. Similarly, Talmon's theory will be of little help to anyone seeking to explain "rightist totalitarian" regimes in Italy, Spain, and Portugal or a rightist military, corporatist regime like Brazil's, Argentina's, or Chile's. By no stretch of the imagination can messianic orientations be conjured up for Fascist Italy, Franco's Spain, or such ideologically philistine regimes as those of Brazil, Argentina, and Egypt. No one could describe the cynicism of the present technocratic Soviet leadership as "political messianism." Indeed, the Soviet leaders are no more an elite exclusively engaged in the pursuit of truth politics than Stalin's gulag camps were reformatory agencies of the bolshevik secular religion. Mao's messianism is the exception, but it has not been adopted by his successors.

58. Talmon, *The Rise of Totalitarian Democracy*, pp. 1–11.

Arendt's brilliant analysis of totalitarianism has yielded powerful insights into the political goals and behavior of the nazi and
bolshevik movements. She was among the first to point out that
racism and anti-Semitism were Hitler's foremost concerns and
that they played a key role in the politics of his auxiliary-
praetorian instrument, the SS. The profundity of Arendt's statement that "Nazism and Bolshevism owe more to Pan-Germanism
and Pan-Slavism (respectively) than to any other ideology or political movement"[59] is obvious. And yet her thesis that modern authoritarianism, which she calls totalitarianism, was founded on a
classless society is totally incorrect. In fact, the USSR is the preeminent class society. The regime is bureaucratic, technocratic, and
managerial, thus resembling a modern corporation. What is total
in the USSR is the party's aspirations and ideology, which have
little to do with either mass society or class conflict. Arendt's thesis
actually makes it more difficult to explain empirically the nature,
structure, and behavior of Nazi Germany and the USSR. Capitalist
bourgeois economics actually flourished under the Nazis, and the
bureaucratic, centralized party-state of the USSR was established
at the expense of the mass society.[60]

There is more evidence, of course. Allen and Peterson refute the
argument that Germany was a totalitarian state.[61] Solzhenitsyn's
Gulag Archipelago graphically shows that the torture system of the
Stalinist state more closely approximates classical historical
tyranny—corrupt, vindictive, and oppressive rule—than a party-
aided effort to mold the masses in the bolshevik ideological image.
Neither Stalin's autocratic rule nor Hitler's despotism demonstrates "mob rule" or ideological rule. In fact, the apparatchiks of
the gulags and of the Final Solution were efficient, modern
technocrats, specialists in assassination and torture, who were
trained in the auxiliary political structures. They definitely were

59. Arendt, *The Origins of Totalitarianism*, p. 222.
60. On the economy of Nazi Germany, see Alan Milward, *The German
Economy at War* (London: Athlone Press, 1965); and Arthur Schweitzer, *Big
Business in the Third Reich* (Bloomington: Indiana University Press, 1964).
61. William S. Allen, *The Nazi Seizure of Power* (Chicago: Quadrangle,
1965); and Edward Peterson, *The Limits of Hitler's Power* (Princeton, N.J.:
Princeton University Press, 1968).

not dedicated to the fulfillment of the masses' appetite for political organization. Mussolini's Italy, Franco's Spain, corporatist and praetorian Brazil, Nasserite Egypt—none of the most representative authoritarian regimes of modern times have been mass societies or embodiments of ideological rule.

The concept of totalitarianism, as we have remarked, has had several parents, including Mussolini who coined the term, and the demonological school of Arendt, Friedrich, and Talmon. The concept has been revived recently by a political sociologist who is a keen student of Spain, Juan J. Linz.* Linz believes, if I am not misinterpreting him, that ideology of mobilization and absolute and sincere commitment are fundamental to the totalitarian ideologue. They make up his operational credo, whatever its political and dynamic adaptations. Totalitarianism is an achievable goal for such individuals; they are motivated and stimulated by the reality of the concept. Totalitarianism also means coercion of the centrality of political power and the emergence of a political elite, a "totalitarian class," for whom totalitarianism is also a workable ideal. The function of totalitarianism is revolutionary, that is, the politicization of society. Totalitarian ideology was the essential source of legitimacy and the popular credo of the masses in Nazi Germany and in the USSR during the early decades of bolshevism.

I have no quarrel with Linz's definition provided one does not question the motivations of Mussolini, Hitler, Ramos, Panunzio, Rosenberg, and other totalitarian ideologues, intellectuals, and politicians. But I do challenge the utility of the concept in explaining the political dynamics of totalitarianism. Mussolini, Hitler, Lenin and Stalin confidently believed in totalitarian solutions and in the ultimate success of totalitarian systems. This does not mean that they achieved it or that it could be accomplished. After all, they have left a legacy of authoritarian instruments: the single authoritarian party, the political police, and the parallel and auxiliary structures in charge of mobilization and control. But this inquiry goes beyond what these men said, what they believed, and

---

*Linz and I had a wonderful marathon discussion of the concept for several nights in New Haven late in April 1979. I am most grateful for the time Linz spent "educating" me and correcting errors in my manuscript, although, of course, we did not always agree.

where they were headed. I have assumed that totalitarianism is fundamentally and intellectually chimeric; the relation between totalitarian instruments is not relative, and the concept is tautological. To explain the dynamics of modern authoritarianism I must first establish the importance of the relationships between its political structures.

Totalitarianism does not explain the dynamics of either its structures or its systems. To be meaningfully considered, these dynamics must be seen as authoritarian, not totalitarian. Bolshevism in its various forms still exists because the Leninist model was not really totalitarian. We could also speculate that neither the nazi nor the fascist regimes would have endured as totalitarian systems. The craving for "totalitarianism" is greater at the outset of any regime than during its development. To deal with this political evolution, I will establish periods in its sequence. Neither bolshevism nor fascism could be expected to retain the vigor, creativity, enthusiasm, and support in later years as in decades earlier. In fact, if the evolution of bolshevism from Lenin via Mao to Castro and Vietnam demonstrates anything, it is that the mantle of originality, virginity, and idealistic vigor has passed from the cynical post-Brezhnev USSR to Vietnam and Cuba.

Another element of totalitarianism concerns the circumstances under which it (in Linz's sense) emerged. The bolsheviks had to begin almost from the essentials—the patrimonial, venal, and inefficient czarist regime had collapsed, leaving behind a country torn by warring nationalists, an imperialistic and counterrevolutionary civil war, and an elemental peasant mass revolt. The Nazis, in contrast, inherited an orderly regime, an efficient Prussian-German bureaucracy, a rehabilitated military, and a working economic and political system. However, the nation was divided. The left and the right had never reconciled; they had merely coexisted after 1925 under a prosperous Weimar regime. Though the disparities between the powerful blocs of the left and the Nazis were significant, there was no civil war. Hitler thus had a better electoral start than Lenin and Stalin. Mussolini inherited both a defeated nation, which bore the scars of Capareto and Fiume, and the remnants of the corrupt and ineffective Giolittian parliamentary regime. The

Fascists exploited the demise not only of the liberal state but of its ideology.

In his comparative study "Totalitarian and Authoritarian Regimes," Juan Linz proposes that an authoritarian system is totalitarian if it has the following attributes:

a. a monistic but not monolithic center of power
b. an exclusive, autonomous, and more or less intellectually elaborate ideology that serves to legitimize the leader's power
c. citizen participation and active mobilization for political and collective social tasks.[62]

Linz's version of totalitarianism is distinguished from authoritarian systems by the use of ideology as an instrument of legitimation. Totalitarian systems possess an exclusive ideology while authoritarian systems lack an "elaborate and guiding ideology, with distinctive mentalities [sic]."[63] In principle, I have no quarrel with Linz. However, the political, institutional, and structural behavior of so-called totalitarian regimes does not exhibit this preeminent role of the ultimate ideology. The formation of political structures in totalitarian systems demonstrates great concern for protecting ideology, but only in order to safeguard the ruling elite and its institutions. In most, if not all, totalitarian systems, ideology is not the motor that propels the regime, the state, and the society; Linz himself supports this in all his writings. Pragmatism guides the leadership, especially as the regime becomes more mature and more institutionalized. To defend the totalitarian model, one must demonstrate that ideology, through the party, provides a continuous and essential link between the regime, the state, and the society.

The only modern systems that have approximated Linz's totalitarian model for any substantial period of time are the USSR under Stalin, the People's Republic of China in Mao's late years,

62. Juan Linz, "Totalitarian and Authoritarian Regimes," in *Handbook of Political Science*, ed. F. Greenstein and N. Polsby (Reading, Mass.: Addison-Wesley, 1975), vol. 3, *Macropolitical Theory*, pp. 175–412.
63. Ibid., p. 264.

and Communist Vietnam since 1972. In Nazi Germany, on the other hand, the racist and nationalist ideology did not always link the regime to the state, the party, and the society. Instead, it coercively legitimized the Hitler dictatorship. Italy, too, was a far cry from this conception of totalitarianism. Establishing a typology on the foundations of Hitlerism, Leninism, Stalinism, and Maoism only correctly identifies these regimes' exploitation of their secular religions. The nazi ideology can explain the concepts and patterns of belief that purport to explain complex social phenomena in Germany, but Arendt's "totalitarian ideology as an explanatory function" largely fails to account for the evolution of institutional and political structures and relationships in this case.

Next, I cannot identify a single motivation that will explain the "totality" of totalitarianism. In a totalitarian analysis, what was nazism? Was it radical nationalism, a drive for a racist utopia, a pan-Germanic movement, an imperialist doctrine, Hitler's political system, Himmler's police state, or a combination of all of these? After all, Nyomarkay has argued persuasively that nazi ideology did not serve as an arbiter of nazism.[64]

But Hitler was the incarnation of nazism. The hypothesis that nazism would have collapsed if Hitler had been removed (unless the political police had taken over) is more plausible than that Marxist communism could survive the departure of Lenin, Stalin, Mao, Ho, and Castro. It is doubtful that it would endure in Poland or Czechoslovakia without Soviet enforcement. If ideology provides the raison d'être for party, state, regime, and individuals in Bolshevik systems, it is clear that in practice no singular interpretation of Marxism emerges. Bolshevism had no führer. The Nazi party before 1933 might have been relegated to the dustbin of history. Why not after Hitler's death?

Linz's third requirement for modern totalitarianism is the mobilization of citizen participation for collective goals. The bolshevik and fascist ideologies both served this function. Although the single totalitarian party should also fulfill this purpose, only bolshevik parties have done so, despite Linz's contention that "only

64. Joseph Nyomarkay, *Charisma and Factionalism in the Nazi Party* (Minneapolis: University of Minnesota Press, 1967), pp. 3–6.

when the party organization is superior or equal to the government can we speak of a totalitarian system."[65] In fact, Lenin, Stalin, Hitler, and Mao were tyrants and sometimes ruled without regard to party, ideology, or society, although they exploited ideology to legitimize their domination. Ideology survived all of them, because authoritarian institutions proved more powerful than tyrants.

The fact that some totalitarian systems have pluralistic institutional structures is politically irrelevant. The pluralism that exists within the ruling elite's bureaucratic politics explains only methods of policy-making. Political domination is determined by patterns of political recruitment. Bureaucratic squabbles only emphasize the secondary role played by bureaucratic and administrative elites in the power system. But even this type of pluralism is rare. Since, as Linz points out, many authoritarian systems do not have "extensive or intensive political mobilization,"[66] and they are noncohesive, noninstitutionalized political entities, the chance for pluralism to emerge within a cohesive ruling elite is dim indeed. Thus, once more, the institutional nature of the polity and its political arrangements, not its ideology, determines its nature and structure. The absence or existence of a monistic elite does not make the system more or less totalitarian but more or less authoritarian. What characterizes most, if not all, modern authoritarian systems is that they are one-party or partyless regimes. The modern nondemocratic state is an authoritarian state, which is more or less effective, more or less brutal, and usually operates through plebiscites rather than by fully mobilizing the population.

Although I am able to discern some parallels between Linz's and my approach to the subject (and I am certainly in debt to Linz's superior analysis of Spanish corporatism), I cannot completely accept his definition of totalitarianism. I still regard the concept of totalitarianism as a metaphysical and intellectual creation of both fascist writers and their most bitter antagonists. In Brzezinski's view, totalitarianism is "explicitly or implicitly . . . a tendency toward the destruction of the lines between state and society and the emergence of 'total' politicization of society by politi-

---

65. Linz, "Totalitarian and Authoritarian Regimes," p. 212.
66. Ibid., p. 104.

cal organizations, generally the party and its affiliates."[67] In my
view, this definition at best applies only to the bolshevik model
under Stalin. Even Linz's modified definition mistakenly extends
the Soviet model of authoritarianism to other examples. Furthermore, the adaptation of that model by the Soviet Union and
China represents a considerable modification of the bolshvik concept of total politicization. Thus, authoritarianism remains a more
realistic working concept for exploring the dynamic relationships
between regime, state, party, and society in authoritarian systems.

Next to the police state, the party-state is the ultimate authoritarian state, not because it is (according to Linz) monistic, exclusive, ideological, and mobilizational but because the party in
the USSR like the SS in Germany, is the most efficient instrument
of authoritarianism. The differences between monolithic and
monistic authority, autonomous and nonautonomous ideology,
and active and less active political participation determine the degree and scope of authoritarianism. Thus, the Bolshevik party and
the Nazi SS proved to be more efficient, resilient, innovative, and
successful instruments of authoritarianism than the comparable
institutions in, for example, corporatist Brazil and Nasserite Egypt.

In the Nazi state, ideology became instrumental after 1934.
During the war, Goebbels used ideology to mobilize the society,
making Germany a more cohesive and efficient war machine. Hitler himself revived the party in order to win the war. But nazi
ideology eventually began to lose its power to mobilize the people
(except, of course, for anti-Semitism and racism, which were fundamental tenets, although peripheral to the domination of the
German state and society). Soviet ideology in the 1980s no longer
mobilizes masses nor is a system of the permanent purge. In Italy,
fascist ideology lost its substance, eventually becoming a super-
Italian nationalist ideology in the service of economic modernization.

Although ideology can provide the initial momentum for a revolutionary movement and enhance a regime's efficiency in mobilizing human resources, it is neither a fundamental nor a permanent
requirement for the development of authoritarianism. In fact, in

67. Ibid., p. 187.

the Soviet Union today, authoritarian legitimacy is enhanced more by creating stable authoritarian structures than by attending to ideology. Totalitarian analysis cannot explain why the SS police state was in ascendance as nazi ideology ebbed. Certainly the USSR and China continue to become more efficient and stable while bolshevik ideology decays. In China, though the decline of ideology is less pronounced, the same assertion applies. Nazi Germany, the ultimate authoritarian state, was "without extensive or intensive political mobilization" except during the seizure of power and during the mobilization effort dictated by total war.[68]

Authors of the totalitarian school confuse the eras in which the new authoritarian system dedicates itself to a total war against a former regime or an imaginary new opposition with periods when the regime can function without resorting to repression. The "totalitarian" era of authoritarianism occurs principally during the seizure of power or during periods of enforced regeneration such as the Zhdanovite and Maoist cultural revolutions. Once the revolutionary dust has settled, the regime and its political structures seek stability. This development portends ideological decline.

I should emphasize that I do not consider ideology to be mere window dressing. Certainly the ideological continuum is time-linked. Thus, although ideology for the Bolshevik, Nazi, and Fascist founding fathers was primary and all-encompassing, it is not so for their successors in the USSR, or, for that matter, in Poland, Czechoslovakia, and Hungary. In post-Tito Yugoslavia, ideology will not cause either cohesion or disintegration; Tito's successors view communism as an instrument, an attitude that demands little conviction or dedication.[69]

William LeoGrande argues that an ideological distinction between left and right serves an institutional purpose and that I have reduced authoritarian ideology to its instrumental function.[70] This may be so. Unquestionably the task of rightist authoritarianism—to eliminate its opponents—has dynamic political and institutional

68. Ibid., p. 204.
69. Rusinow, *The Yugoslav Experiment*, pp. 192–342.
70. At this point, I should like to thank my colleague William Leo-Grande for his patient reading of this study and his most valuable advice on Cuba.

implications. Thus rightist and leftist authoritarian regimes monopolize and justify power differently. They also clearly represent different types of mobilization, social stratification, and linkages between state and society. Leftist authoritarians might be characterized as more interventionist and less tolerant of unnatural social classes. Leftists integrate, exile, or destroy existing social classes in an attempt to guarantee that their changes will be irreversible. Authoritarians of the right face a cruel dilemma. To achieve their goal of maintaining the existing order, they seek to monopolize political power in the name of a rightist ideology. Therefore they must seek to coerce or persuade the left to support them, even as the left is trying to destroy the existing order in the name of leftist ideology.

Yet the success of the party-state is not dependent on its ideological commitments even though ideology is one political weapon in the seizure of power or in regeneration of a decaying modern autocracy. Instead the party-state depends on the instruments of political power, of which ideology is one. Even if Leninism were pure Marxism, one could advance the argument that its success came about through Stalinization, bureaucratization, and effective use of the party-state and its legal, paralegal, and auxiliary structures. The decline of the Nazi party and the rise of Hitler's political police (as well as the Cultural Revolution in China) support the argument that ideology is necessary to regenerate the authoritarian system and to repeatedly mobilize the people. Nevertheless, the seizure, regeneration and conduct of both leftist and rightist authoritarianism depend in the long run on authoritarian political structures and not on ideology.

Once one disposes of the totalitarian school's devil theory of politics, authoritarian regimes and movements must be explained in *political* terms. The evolution and success of the Nazi and Bolshevik parties bear witness to the achievements of Hitler and Lenin. Each was a consummate politican, and each, with Mussolini, was an innovator of modern political procedures, institutions, and structures. Each won his political battles by determined and brilliant use of the instruments of modern politics—mass parties, propaganda, oratory, agitation, political mobilization, new electoral techniques (Hitler's use of the airplane contributed to the electoral success of the Nazis), and innovative auxiliary and parallel political structures.[71] The Nazis had no monopoly on anti-Semitism, racism, radical nationalism, anticapitalism, national socialism and antiforeignism; many of these ideas predated them. The Nazis' rivals on the right, Hugenberg's conservatives, the Stalhelm, the Munich patriotic societies, the conservative anti-Semitic parties, the Freikorps, the Bayern Bund, and the various ultranationalist, racist and anti-Semitic groups were as vehement and successful in exploiting these themes as were Hitler and the Nazis. On the left the communists and the left-wing socialists appealed to working- and middle-class constituencies similar to those of the Nazis.[72] Both right-wing and left-wing political parties and movements employed large-scale paramilitary forces, agitation, and propaganda techniques. Hitler's behavior, his party's tactics, and his ideas were not significantly different from those of his opponents. They all reviled the traitors of Berlin and the polluters of the so-called Aryan race with equal vehemence. Yet Hitler won, not the conservatives, the socialists, Hugenberg, Von Papen, or the paramilitary rovers. Hitler's skills as an orator, propagandist, and party organizer were important, but his victory was largely the result of his brilliant political skills (for example, his manipulation of the right, the Reichswehr, the Hindenburg Court, Von Papen and Von Schleicher in 1932–1933), which he exercised through the modern mobilizing party and auxiliary structures he had built since 1921. The new literature on Hitler's rise to power and the evolution of the Nazi party definitely demonstrates that Hitler won playing by the rules of Weimar politics.[73]

71. For a revisionist interpretation of Hitler's rise to power, and an explanation of why the Nazis did better than their rivals, see William Carr, *Hitler: A Study in Personality and Politics* (London: Edward Arnold, 1978), pp. 1–39.

72. For bibliography of leftist and rightist parties, movements and paramilitary groups see Peter Stachura, ed., *The Shaping of the Nazi State* (London: Croom Helm, 1978); James Diehl, *Paramilitary Politics in Weimar Germany* (Bloomington: Indiana University Press, 1977); and John Leopold, *Alfred Hugenberg: The Radical Nationalist Campaign against the Weimar Republic* (New Haven: Yale University Press, 1977).

73. See William Carr, *Hitler*; and D. Orlow, *History of the Nazi Party, 1919–1933* (Pittsburgh: University of Pittsburgh Press, 1969).

Lenin's success followed a pattern similar to Hitler's. Lenin's revolutionary ideas were also in the ideological arsenal of the Mensheviks, the Social Revolutionaries and even the Socialists. Russian socialism, anarchism, and revolutionary zeal were a century old before Lenin, a true heir to Herzen and Chernyshevsky, became active.[74] Yet as John Keep aptly writes, whatever Lenin's merits as a philosopher, historian or literary critic, he was preeminently a politician, and it was as a master of political tactics, who skillfully manipulated men and ideas to achieve power for his party, that he won his greatest success.[75]

Lenin's tactics—the elimination of leftist rivals and the seizure of power—destroyed the moderate constitutionalist regime. But Russian bolshevism owes its establishment and longevity to Lenin's political innovations—the party-state, the professional revolutionary elite, the agitation machinery, and the Leninist-Stalinist purgatory. An examination of Chinese communist and Cuban communist experience provides additional support for the contention that the skillful use of political power, not ideology, determines the success and failures of modern authoritarian leaders and political structures.

The partial successes of Mussolini, Nasser, Perón, and other praetorian and corporative rulers are also linked to their employment of modern political strategies and procedures to gain and sustain political power. All have been concerned with political mobilization, economic modernization, and the employment of political techniques to fulfill their goals and aspirations. The corporative rulers Franco and Salazar proved more successful in sustaining political power than the new corporative praetorians. In my view their success results mainly from political skills, in which most Latin American and Third World military leaders are notori-

---

74. Leonard Shapiro, *The Origins of Communist Autocracy* (Cambridge, Mass.: Harvard University Press, 1966); Richard Pipes, "Lenin" in *Revolutionary Russia*, ed. Richard Pipes (Cambridge, Mass.: Harvard University Press, 1968) pp. 28–62; Leonard Shapiro and Peter Reddaway, eds., *Lenin: The Man, the Theorist, the Leader* (London: Pall Mall, 1967); Philip Selznick, *The Organizational Weapon* (Glencoe, Ill.: Free Press, 1952).

75. John Keep, "Lenin as a Tactician," in *Lenin*, ed. Shapiro and Reddaway, p. 135.

ously deficient.[76] A military organization is not the best school for training in politics. The inability of the authoritarian praetorian (corporate, oligarchic, and particularly tyrannical) regimes to create and sustain political and auxiliary structures is one reason for their failure. Officers who prove to possess political skills certainly survive longer in power. Nasser, Sadat, Assad, and Saadam Hussein are typical, and Kemal Ataturk of Turkey is the outstanding example of a politically able military praetorian who created relatively viable political structures.

Marxism and Fascism

Marxism and fascism, the most conspicuous modern revolutionary and authoritarian ideologies, gave birth to modern authoritarian political structures. The connection, intellectual affinity, and antagonism between Marxism and fascism has been demonstrated recently in the writings of A. James Gregor.[77] Using a novel approach, Gregor argues that the crisis in Marxism, especially the severe dilemmas posed for Marxist intellectuals by the nature of revolutionary consciousness, notably that of the proletariat, paved the way for paradigmatic fascism. The essence of pragmatic Marxism is that revolutionary action, motivated by the class consciousness that stimulates its antibourgeois revolutionary spirit, is the proletariat's historical mission. As both Lenin and Mussolini discovered, however, revolution is not the natural phenomenon Engels claimed it was, and the proletariat's inclinations are nonrevolutionary.[78] This revealed serious weaknesses in Marx's theory of collective psychology (class consciousness) and in his economic analysis (the inevitability of the collapse of capitalism).[79]

Classical Marxism ignored two of the modern world's most im-

76. See Perlmutter, *The Military and Politics in Modern Times*, chaps. 5, 6.

77. A. James Gregor, *The Fascist Persuasion in Radical Politics*, chaps. 4, 5. See also A. James Gregor, *The Ideology of Fascism* (New York: Free Press, 1969).

78. Gregor, *The Fascist Persuasion in Radical Politics*, pp. 86–138.

79. Ibid., pp. 139–53.

portant social, political, and ideological realities—nationalism and
the resilience of the modern nation-state. Marx viewed historical
nationalism as moribund, and the nation-state as no more than
the executive of collapsing imperialistic capitalism. As Gregor puts
it, "Neither Marx nor Engels conceived nationalism as having any
independent historical and social significance."[80] Nevertheless, the
issue has preoccupied Marxist theoreticians, politicians, and revolutionaries throughout this century.[81] Gregor argues that both
Lenin and Mussolini found different, but not essentially dissimilar,
solutions to this painful dilemma. Both opted for elitist and statist
solutions.[82]

Lenin insisted that the "proletariat, left to its own devices,
would remain forever venal."[83] His strategy was, therefore,
minoritarian. The party replaced class, and the elitist party-state
replaced the proletarian vanguard, which now was represented by
the dictatorship of the proletariat.[84] Bolshevism was authoritarian,
nationalistic, and etatist from the very beginning:

> "By the time the Bolshevik revolution matured into a viable
> political system, classical Marxism had been transformed into a
> legitimizing rationale for a developmental and autarchic
> nationalism, energized by a self-selected and self-perpetuating
> leadership that wielded the complex apparatus of a bureaucratic
> state in the service of human and natural resource mobilization,
> allocation, and control."[85]

80. Ibid., p. 88.
81. On Marxism and nationalism, see Shlomo Avineri, *Karl Marx on
Colonialism and Modernization* (Garden City, N.Y.: Doubleday, 1966), pp.
1–28; Karl Marx, *The Eastern Question* (London: Swan Sonnenschein,
1897); Edward Bernstein, *Evolutionary Socialism* (New York: Schoken,
1961); V. I. Lenin, *What Is To Be Done?* (New York: International Publishers, 1953); Shlomo Avineri, *The Social and Political Thought of Karl Marx*
(Cambridge: At the University Press, 1968); and H. B. David, *Nationalism
and Socialism* (New York: Monthly Review, 1961).
82. Gregor, *The Fascist Persuasion in Radical Politics*, pp. 111–34.
83. Ibid., p. 113.
84. Ibid., p. 122.
85. Ibid., pp. 132–33. See also J. H. Keep, *The Russian Revolution* (New
York: Norton, 1976); Shapiro, *The Origins of Communist Autocracy;* and J.
E. Connor, *Lenin: On Politics and Revolution* (New York: Pegasus, 1968).

Lenin's solution was organizational and bureaucratic. In *What Is To Be Done?*, Lenin, inspired as he was by the Jacobins of the 1870s, made a clear distinction between the "organization of revolutionaries" and the "organization of workers." He "rejected the suggestion that there was any theoretical affinity between Bolshevism and Popularism."[86] Firmly in the Russian radical tradition, Lenin was an elitist. His distrust of the nonrevolutionary nature of the proletariat was not so much a result of practical experience with workers, but an intellectual residue of Russian and European radicalism. Long before Lenin realized that social democracy eventually would assume power, he had become deeply suspicious of its readiness to deal with the essentially nonrevolutionary proletariat. Thus his concepts of party organization and the state were formed quite early in the century, and they persisted throughout his career as revolutionary, statesman, and dictator. The outline of Lenin's party-state, the concept of Bolshevik elitism, the nexus of party, state, and revolution, all stem from the radical tradition and from Lenin's obsession with centralism and control and with suppressing the nonrevolutionary and democratic elements within the party and the state. As John Keep put it, "The emergence of a mass labour movement did not in his [Lenin's] view require the revolutionaries to make a fundamental change in their organizational techniques, but on the contrary made centralism more essential than ever."[87]

Early in his career as both a Marxist and a socialist, Mussolini also became aware of the nonrevolutionary nature of the proletariat. He became convinced "that the revolution involved not only the calculation of the material interst of men and classes but an invocation of *sentiment* as well."[88] In the sociological tradition of Pareto (an antifascist), Michels (a nonfascist), and Sorel, Mussolini transferred the "sentiment of solidarity" from the class to the masses and transformed class consciousness into nationalist consciousness and solidarity.[89] A radical Marxist, Mussolini, like Len-

86. John Keep, *The Rise of Social Democracy in Russia* (Oxford: Clarendon Press, 1963), p. 94.
87. Ibid., pp. 94–95.
88. Gregor, *The Fascist Persuasion in Radical Politics*, p. 144.
89. Ibid.

in, opted for minoritarianism. Mussolini, however, chose the syndicalist concept of elitism rather than the Leninist party-state solution. A mixture of Sorel's violence, Pareto's elitism and Le Bon's mob psychology served as the foundation for Mussolini's paradigmatic fascism, which encompassed associationism, militancy, minoritarianism and anti-individualism. All of these were anchored in "paralogical and sentimental appeals" and were mixed with Italian radical nationalism.[90] Fascism also was transformed by its syndicalist variant of authoritarianism and by the rise of the psychology of the Veterans of the War, that is, the "warrior intellectuals" and "the generation of the front" (later the *Kaderprinzip* of the German Free Corps). War, nationalism, and authoritarianism were to counter the nonrevolutionary nature of bourgeois society. Nationalism would provide the needed revolutionary consciousness and solidarity.

Despite the ideological differences between bolshevism, fascism, and nazism, their Marxist origins (even if German volkism differed from Russian nationalism) are as clear as their authoritarian orientations. The party-state model and its fascist variants can be explained in terms of post-Marxist solutions: the elitist, authoritarian takeover of the machinery of the state and the creation of auxiliary and parallel political structures to buttress regimes that operate in the absence of a revolutionary proletarian consciousness. In other words, all party, police, and corporatist systems were designed, in recognition of the absence of continuous mass and proletarian revolutionary orientations, to serve as the developmental dictatorships of mobilization.

The Ideology of Modern Authoritarianism

Modern authoritarianism does not feed on metaphysical conceptions of history. In the ideology of *all* modern authoritarian movements, parties, and regimes five elements converge: radical nationalism; antiliberalism; antiparliamentarism; an antibourgeois ethos; and anti-Semitism and racism.

90. Ibid., pp. 154–82.

Radical Nationalism

Nationalism is the most powerful instrument of mass mobilization for all modern authoritarian regimes. Although they paid lip service to Marx's internationalism, even the bolsheviks used the theory of capitalist encirclement—borne out by intervention during the 1918–1920 civil war—to tap nationalistic support. And the Soviets officially designated the four years of war with Hitler's Germany as the Great Patriotic War.

Hitler's most powerful appeal was his total dedication to radical nationalism. He consistently used two rallying cries to advance the Nazi movement. One was the "stab in the back" idea, which played upon the German electorate's categorical commitment to the theory that the Versailles treaty had been designed to reduce Germany to the status of a minor state and thus was responsible for Germany's economic ills and political plight. Unquestionably, however, the Nazis' most significant contribution to the German nationalist movement was the resurrection of racial theories. The essence of Hitlerian anti-Semitism was racism. The call for the cleansing of Germany, which meant the removal of its Jewish citizens, created powerful support for the Nazis.[91]

Fascism, to the degree that it can be called an autonomous ideology, was a purely nationalist "philosophy," one of the most prominent radical nationalist theories of modern times. Although the Italian Nationalist and the Fascist parties clashed, the cry for nationalist and cultural regeneration was the most powerful appeal of the squadristi.[92] Both radical and monarchical Fascists conceived the political struggle in terms of nationalist neo-Darwinism and cultural elitism. The defeat of 1918 was a fundamental stimulus to the Italian student movements, which contributed strongly to early fascism.[93] Mussolini's Mediterranean empire building, which brought to fruition an age-old dream held by quasinationalists in the nineteenth century, represented an even

91. George L. Mosse, *The Crisis of German Ideology: Intellectual Origins of the Third Reich* (New York: Grosset and Dunlap, 1964).
92. See Adrian Lyttleton, *The Seizure of Power.*
93. In my analysis I depend heavily on Adrian Lyttleton, *The Seizure of Power.* See especially p. 17.

greater lure to the new fascist nationalists. "Mussolini's regime
came to stand for patriotism, militarism, and anti-Bolshevism."[94]

In the Catholic and fundamentalist corporatism of Franco's
Spain and Salazar's Portugal, nationalism did not play as important a role as it did in Germany and Italy. In Spain, nationalism
was weakened by strong regionalist sentiments. These regimes
(especially Franco's) therefore preferred to suppress local
separatist movements in the name of authoritarianism and benevo-
lent corporatist rule. Franco's nationalism was not romantic; it
sought unity, which meant an end to regionalism, above nationality. Franco did not seek to awaken Spanish nationalism because he
essentially viewed it as the ideology of his opposition in the Civil
War. Because Spanish nationalism was tainted with liberalism,
Spain was not allowed to produce the powerful nationalist electorate that appeared in France, Italy, and Germany. Rather than de-
pending on nationalist mass appeal, Franco's monarchical and
traditional tyranny achieved political control by harnessing social
and economic forces to corporatist etatism. Therefore, while the
Franco dictatorship was not a modern mass polity, its corporatist
ideology was modern.

Unquestionably, nationalism represents the only ideological
link between the military praetorians, whether tyrannical, oligarchic, or corporatist. The Comtism and positivism adopted by the
early praetorians in Argentina and Brazil[95] at the end of the
nineteenth century were superseded in the 1930s by fascism, which
captured the imagination of radical nationalists in the Chilean military as well.[96] Most, if not all, coups in the major Latin American
countries were and are nationalist and corporatist in orientation.
However, since the 1960s, the fear of Castroism has added a wrinkle
to authoritarianism common to Brazil, Argentina and Chile.[97]

Xenophobic and radical nationalism is still the platform of
modern oligarchic praetorians in the Middle East and North Africa. Over 95 percent of the military coups in the Middle East be-

94. Dennis Mack Smith, *Mussolini's Roman Empire* (New York: Viking
Press, 1976), p. 2.
95. Perlmutter, *Military and Politics in Modern Times*, pp. 177–83.
96. Ibid.
97. Ibid.

tween 1936 and 1976 were initiated and executed by civilian-military coalitions of radical, antiforeign nationalists. The xenophobic strain began with numerous Iraqi coups between 1936 and 1941 and continued through the Nasser regime to popular nationalist and the Ba'athi-Syrian military regimes in the 1950s and since 1966. Syria and especially Iraq are still under the influence of virulent xenophobes.

Antiliberalism

Antiliberalism might be called the twin of radical nationalism. In fact, the only distinction between antiliberals and radical nationalists is that they are committed to different types of authoritarianism.

Liberalism, a concept of human enlightenment and of unfettered development and self-expression, is adamantly opposed by the primitive and deterministic postulates of Nazi racist theories and Marxist class determinism.[98] Hitler and the Nazis equated it with the Weimar Republic and its coalition of centrists and moderate socialists. To the Nazis, therefore, liberalism spelled the decline of authority, the demise of national glory, the loss of territory, and surrender to the traitors who accepted the shameful Versailles arrangements. Modern authoritarian regimes in general rule partially mobilized and policed masses. Such systems are diametrically opposed to a political philosophy that is dedicated to lifting the burden of coercion and proclaiming the dignity of man and the inalienable rights of the individual.

Furthermore, liberalism's practical implications include the struggle against the despotic state, which is the pedestal of modern authoritarianism. Similarly, the concepts of minimal state intervention and laissez faire are unacceptable to modern authoritarians. It is most significant that modern authoritarianism has prospered in states where a tradition of liberty and a liberal political ideology were essentially nonexistent (czarist Russia), fragile

98. Guido De Ruggiero, *The History of European Liberalism* (New York: Macmillan, 1926); and *Encyclopedia of the Social Sciences* (New York: Macmillan, 1937) s.v. "Liberalism."

(monarchical and Bismarckian Prussia), or tainted by corruption (Giolittian Italy). The weakness of the liberal tradition in most of Latin America is well known, and liberalism has never gained a foothold throughout most of the Middle East and sub-Saharan Africa, where praetorian authoritarianism has flourished. Although Egypt and Syria did have liberal-constitutionalist parties between 1920 and 1950, they were not very important politically.

Antiparliamentarism

Antiliberalism is also a close companion of antiparliamentarism. Fascist Italy is a prime example. The Italian nationalists "shared common ground with Mussolini in a hostility to democracy and parliament," writes Smith.[99] Lyttleton's major thesis is that the crisis of the liberal state in Italy was the product of a revolt against Giolitti's corrupt and decadent parliamentarism.[100] The fascists blamed the liberals and the parliamentary regime for Italian losses in World War I and took malicious joy in the demise of the liberal state.

Lenin's early career contains many graphic illustrations of his contempt for parliamentarism and for competitive political parties. From the split with the Mensheviks in 1903 through his struggles against Bernstein's version of parliamentary social democracy and Luxemburg's autocratic party, Lenin brought all his intellectual vigor and political might to bear against parties, parliaments, and other such appurtenances of bourgeois capitalism. This opposition culminated in his ruthless annihilation of opposition in the soviets and the minoritarian takeover of the government.

The major characteristic of modern praetorianism in the Middle East, Asia, and Africa is its deep contempt for parliamentarism and party government, which are considered tools of colonial rule and have been denounced as corrupt, irresponsible, reactionary, and contrary to, for example, the "Arab spirit." This attitude was reflected by one of the leading Arab praetorians, Gamal Abdel Nasser. "The dictatorship from which we have suffered under the

99. Smith, *Mussolini's Roman Empire*, p. 2.
100. Lyttleton, *The Seizure of Power*, pp. 15–41.

name of democracy," said Nasser, "was the dictatorship of capital, feudalism, under the name of parliament." He continued:

> Political democracy cannot be a reality unless there is social justice and social democracy and unless there is equal opportunity between the capitalist and the worker and between the feudalist and the agricultural laborer. One has plenty of money and can have a good dinner and one has no money to pay for dinner. Capitalists and feudalists want to hold general elections according to Western methods adopted by capitalist countries in which the minority enjoys all the influence and has an abundance of money. The political parties serve the interests of feudalists and capitalists.[101]

The relationship between praetorianism and parliamentarism is more complex in Latin America. Some countries there have long and respected parliamentary histories. A new government, reluctant to tamper with tradition overtly, may maintain the facade while changing the rules to ensure its control. When the regime does not plan to be in power indefinitely, it may view parliament as an important element in the transition back to civilian and possibly democratic rule.

The Antibourgeois Ethos

The bourgeois may well be *the* major figure of modern history, in particular, the bourgeois who espouses a specific life style. As Zeldin said, "it is not wealth that makes a man a bourgeois, but the way the wealth is acquired and the way it is spent." For example, the bourgeois requires decorum in the tailoring of his clothes and in the preparation and consumption of his food:

> "The bourgeois spent less money than the worker on food. What distinguished him was that he served his food differently, with a tablecloth laid symmetrically, and placed in a special room, not in the kitchen. He had to have a *salon*, furnished with a piano,

101. Amos Perlmutter, *Egypt: The Praetorian State* (New Brunswick, N.J.: Transaction, 1974), p. 139; and Perlmutter, *Military and Politics in Modern Times*, pp. 140, 146, 147–49.

paintings, candelabras, clocks, and bibelots in which to receive visitors, and to show that he possessed a surplus of wealth, dedicated to cultured living, beyond the basic necessities."[102]

The bourgeois, who engages in what Thorstein Veblen long ago called conspicuous consumption, devotes himself to the family, his children's education, and respectability. Adolf Hitler stands as modern tyranny's most illustrious petit bourgeois. Benito Mussolini espoused most of the bourgeois ethos, as does Anwar al-Sadat of Egypt, and countless praetorians in Latin America and the Middle East. Lenin, Stalin, Mao, Ho Chi Minh, fascist intellectuals, and Nasser, however, did not. With the exception of Trotsky, they prefered monastic austerity to bourgeois infatuations.

Despite this variation, modern authoritarian ideology, ethos, and aspirations are vehemently antibourgeois. Although most first-generation Bolsheviks were the children of bourgeoisie, Jews, or lower nobility, they were intellectually and politically the most avid antibourgeois of all times. Lenin's followers called for class warfare against the bourgeoisie, their economics, and their life style. The Fascists' contempt for bourgeois parliamentary politics and capitalist avarice was no less vehement. The austerity, discipline, and pretentious simplicity of some of the military praetorians in Latin America and the Middle East also led them to disdain the bourgeois ethos.

Yet authoritarian rulers and systems have opposed the bourgeois ethos for vastly different reasons. The Russian intelligentsia, for example, who were the children of state bureaucrats and the rural petty nobility, adopted an antibourgeois orientation largely as a reflection of their personal rejection of their parents' life style. In addition, the intellectual laid claim to his role as societal critic largely by demonstrating his disdain for bourgeois niceties, which he viewed as the fruits of accumulation and fraud. Latin American military praetorians in the 1890s preferred to emulate austere Prussian officers rather than merchants, who had little prestige in anticapitalist, Catholic countries. The authoritarian's disrespect for the bourgeois ethic echoes from as far back as Aristo-

102. Many of the ideas that follow this quote were borrowed from Theodore Zeldin, *France 1848–1945* (Oxford: Clarendon Press, 1973), 1:15.

tle's contempt for the timocrat, that is, the bureaucratic tyrant of the merchant and middle classes.

For the Arab military, praetorian martial values, the Ottoman legacy, and sultanist orientations contributed heavily to contempt for merchants, the urban bourgeoisie, and pashas. Because the bankers and pashas of Egypt were seen as the venal corrupters of both Islamic civilization and the spirit of modern Arabism, they became the symbolic targets of Nasser's 1952 coup and are now targets of authoritarian Moslem puritans.

Anti-Semitism and Racism

Anti-Semitism, racism, and anti-internationalism are corollaries of radical nationalism, yet they compose a distinct ideological orientation. Whether combined or separate, these elements significantly influence both the ideology and the policies pursued by authoritarians. Only authoritarian states have made anti-Semitism and racism state doctrines with policy implications. The most overt examples are Nazi Germany (in Italy, Mussolini did not "pragmatically" surrender to Hitler's demands until 1943), the radical praetorian Arab states, and some Latin American praetorian systems. However subtle, racism was a state policy in Mao's China and in the USSR; at the height of Stalinism, it was openly and brutally used to suppress nationalities.

In the USSR, Poland, Hungary, and Czechoslovakia anticosmopolitanism is a euphemism for anti-internationalism. It is also a subtle but nonetheless anti-Semitic policy. Internationalism is perceived as a capitalist, imperialistic and Zionist conspiracy by Syria, Iraq, and Argentina as well as the USSR. These regimes have shared this view at different times, but with equal dedication and commitment.

Although it could be argued that anti-Semitism is not a universal phenomenon of modern authoritarianism, both leftist and rightist authoritarian regimes and movements have espoused an ideology of anti-Semitism, racism, and anticosmopolitanism. Historically, anti-Semitism has been deeply embedded in most East Central European states and in Russia, where rightist authoritarian and nonmobilizatory regimes seized upon the Jews in their

search for internal foes. This anti-Semitic policy was legitimized
by Stalin and the East European Stalinists in the 1950s. A leading
political scientist who studies Eastern and Central Europe, Joseph
Rothschild, points this out. "Indeed, the only potent international
ideology in the area at the time [in East Central Europe between
1919 and 1939] was neither Marxism, on the left hand, nor dynastic
loyalism, on the right, but anti-Semitism based on both conviction
and expedience."[103] During the Stalinist era in the USSR and East
Central Europe, Rothschild adds, "This [anti-Semitism] in turn,
provided an ideological bond and precondition for eventual collab-
oration with the Nazis, including the administration of war time
genocide."[104]

Anti-Semitism is also found in democratic and capitalist systems. But what I refer to here is political anti-Semitism, the official
policy of regimes that employ state and political power to enforce
it. Political anti-Semitism was typical of Nazi Germany and of fascist movements in Central and Southeastern Europe, where the
special position of Jews contributed significantly to the rise of fascism. Although not an official doctrine in the USSR, the anti-
Semitism of Stalinist rule is notorious. In the view of Nazis, Fascists, and Bolsheviks alike, the Jews are the incarnation of
capitalist, liberal, and imperialist democracy.

It is no longer necessary to detail the essential role anti-
Semitism and racism played in the political and intellectual circles
of the Nazi state. Hitler used anti-Semitism to rally peasants, petit
bourgeoisie, and working-class authoritarians to the Nazi banner.
The Final Solution was to be the supreme achievement of the Nazi
regime. During the war it became the raison d'être of the German
state. Himmler used it as a vehicle for the rise of the SS, and if
Hitler had died earlier, it might even have ensured SS domination
of the state apparatus. Although Mussolini was not an anti-Semite,
he eventually succumbed to Hitler's superior will.[105]

103. Joseph Rothschild, *East Central Europe between the Two World
Wars* (Seattle: University of Washington Press, 1977), p. 10.
104. Ibid.
105. The literature on this topic is immense; I shall cite only a few
major references. On Nazi Germany, see Raul Hilberg, *The Destruction of
the European Jews* (Chicago: Quadrangle Books, 1961); Donald J. Niewyk,
The Jews in Weimar Germany (Baton Rouge, La.: Louisiana State University

In the Arab countries, it is an academic exercise to distinguish between anti-Semitism and anti-Zionism; the latter generally is the official state policy. Although Arab countries may tolerate a few Jews, anti-Semitism, which the Arabs inherited from the Ottomans, prevails.[106] Arab anti-Semitism is officially sanctioned and praetorians have produced a considerable body of anti-Semitic and racist literature. The majority of military praetorians in Egypt (Sadat's beliefs on the subject are notorious), Iraq, Libya, and to some extent, Syria, are openly anti-Semitic.[107]

The case of the Bolsheviks is more complex. Although Jewish intellectuals played a conspicuous role in first-generation bolshevism, Marxist writings are replete with anti-Semitism.[108] Not until the 1970s, however, did the Soviet Union actively defend anti-Semitic policies, both domestically and internationally. The USSR's alliance with Arab states and the Jews' struggle to emigrate from the Soviet Union exacerbated tensions between the Soviet Union, the Jews, and Israel. Since then, the Soviet state has permitted wider dissemination of literature that attacks all Jews (not simply Zionists). It has also directly (as in the Ukraine or Belorussia) or indirectly supported anti-Semitism by funding the publication of anti-Semitic literature.

Anti-Semitism is a significant element in radical nationalism and antiliberalism, and regimes whose official doctrines and state policies are dedicated to these ideologies generally are also anti-Semitic. Thus, anti-internationalism also explains the ideology of modern authoritarianism.

Press, 1980), pp. 43–81; and Peter Pulzer, *The Rise of Political Anti-Semitism in Germany and Austria* (New York: Wiley, 1964). On Arab anti-Semitism, see Yehoshafat Harkabi, *The Arab Attitude toward Israel* (Washington: Harar, 1971); and Neville Mandel, *The Arabs and Zionism before World War I* (Berkeley: University of California Press, 1976).

106. Mandel, *The Arabs and Zionism*, pp. 223–31.

107. Harkabi, *The Arab Attitude toward Israel;* Mandel, *The Arabs and Zionism.*

108. Edmund Silberner, *Socialist Anti-Semitism* (Jerusalem: Magnes Press, 1954); S. M. Lipset, *Political Man* (New York: Anchor Doubleday, 1960); on the anti-Semitism of Marx, see Julius Carlebach, *Karl Marx and the Radical Critique of Judaism* (London: Routledge and Kegan Paul, 1978), pp. 148–86.

In summary, modern authoritarian states contemptuously and totally reject the modern liberal's pluralist democratic state. Their most powerful ideological orientations are authoritarian, radical, populist, and nationalist; they are also sometimes racist, anticosmopolitan, and corporatist. As elite-dominated societies, most are dedicated to elite-oriented mobilization in developed countries. Praetorian and corporatist autocracies, on the other hand, favor much more limited political participation.

In short, the effort to distinguish one authoritarian or autocratic regime from another (as the totalitarian model does) on the basis of degree, scope, and level of each regime's commitment to radical nationalism and racism, yields only a *partial* explanation of the politics of modern authoritarianism.

CHAPTER TWO

Political Dynamics

Types of Modern Authoritarian Regimes and Structures

In the following section, I examine the political dynamics of five authoritarian models: bolshevik, nazi, fascist, corporatist, and praetorian.

The Bolshevik Communist Model

Lenin is the author of Soviet authoritarianism, although Trotsky made a considerable contribution, especially to principles of military organization and civil-military relations.[1] After Stalin in-

1. On Lenin's concept of politics, party, and political support, see V. I. Lenin, *The State and the Revolution* (New York: International Publishers, 1951); *What Is To Be Done?* (New York: International Publishers, 1953); *Left Wing Communism* in *Works* (New York: International Publishers, n.d.); and Joseph Stalin, *Problems of Leninism* (Moscow: Marx-Engels-Lenin Institute, 1949). The best interpretative studies of Lenin's political innovations and practices include Adam Ulam, *The Bolsheviks*, (New York: Macmillan, 1965); Leonard Shapiro, *The Origins of Communist Autocracy* (Cambridge, Mass.: Harvard University Press, 1966); Moshe Levin, *Lenin's Last Struggle* (New York: Vintage Books, 1968); R. N. Carew Hunt, *The Theory and Practice of Communism*, rev. ed. (London: Macmillan, 1952), pp. 125–68; Philip Selznick, *The Organizational Weapon* (Glencoe, Ill.: Free Press, 1952). On Lenin's concept of the military party, see L. Trotsky, *History of the Russian Revolution*, trans. Max Eastman (New York: Simon and Schuster, 1939), 1:248–69; Merle Fainsod, *How Russia Is Ruled* (Cambridge, Mass.: Harvard University Press, 1963), pp. 61–62; Fainsod, *Smolensk under Soviet Rule* (Cambridge, Mass.: Harvard University Press, 1958); Julian

stitutionalized Lenin's autocracy through brute force, Khrushchev
and Brezhnev modified it to make bolshevism more palatable to
the Soviet people.

Political Support and Mobilization. Karl Marx was high priest of a
philosophical utilitarianism shorn of its moral commitments to the
capitalist social system. In his analysis of the relationship between
capital and labor, Marx was a theorist of rational organization. In
his practical politics (manifested in the organization of the First
International) and in his trade union and socialist politics, Marx
was an institutionalist. As a Hegelian, he believed that the
dynamics of history could be harnessed and manipulated by the
political organizations of society and the marketplace. Engels
added the principle that ideal society should include the military
organization.

Marx acknowledged the bureaucracy and the military to be the
most potent instruments of the capitalist state, a system he preferred to call "Bonapartism." Engels's "administration of things"
(the socialist state), run by the dictatorship of the proletariat, was
to reverse the relationships between capital and labor; it was not
intended to interfere with the development of a modern economy
but rather to destroy the centralized, bureaucratic state. These
orientations, which were transformed by Lenin and Trotsky, represented a commitment to the rational economic man. After all, what
could be more rational in the Hegelian sense than the socialist
state? In theory it did not exclude corporatism, hierarchy, organization, or legitimacy. Marx and Engels aspired to change the
state's authoritarian relationship, hoping that after the revolution
the state would wither away. Lenin, however, embraced the state,
and his successors adopted its instruments.

By nature, the struggle for power in bolshevism is conspirato-

Towster, *Political Power in the USSR, 1917–1947* (New York: Oxford University Press, 1948); Raymond Bauer, Alex Inkeles, and Clyde Kluckhohn,
How the Soviet System Works (Cambridge, Mass.: Harvard University Press,
1956. See also Nathan Leites, *A Study of Bolshevism* (Glencoe, Ill.: The Free
Press, 1953). On Stalin and his successors, see Seweryn Bialer, *Stalin's Successors: Leadership, Stability and Change in the Soviet Union* (New York:
Cambridge University Press, 1980), pp. 1–126.

rial; it is where the dictatorship of the proletariat and the administration of things merge. Philip Selznick writes:

> Leninism, with its strong emphasis on the power of disciplined
> minorities, affords a most useful case history for the study of
> organizational weapons. At the same time, it is important to
> learn about organizational manipulation if we are fully to com-
> prehend the Bolshevik experience. . . . Using the special role of
> organization as a key, we may expect to learn something about
> the inner dynamics of Bolshevism—that pattern of motivation
> and action which impels it onward to ever-renewed power
> struggles.[2]

Lenin learned a great deal about the apathy and confusion of
the populace and the ultimate impotence of spontaneous revolutions from the collapse of the Paris Commune in 1871 and the
abortive 1905 Russian revolution. Abhorring parliamentarism and
the revisionist social democracy of the Bernstein school, Lenin
opted to secure support by establishing a cohesive party headed by
an executive committee of selected and devoted professional revolutionaries. Since political support from the unconscious proletar-
ians was not expected to provide tinder for Lenin's revolutionary
spark, the burden of the revolution was to be carried by the party's
executive committee. Lenin could not relegate the monumental
task of capturing power by violent insurrection to liberal and social
democratic amateurs. In 1903, he rejected the Russian Social
Democratic Labor party platform for parliamentary assumption of
power, which a minority of Bolsheviks adopted.

The Bolshevik concept was clear—conquest by a revolutionary
party under militant, dedicated professionals. To topple the czarist
state, a well-disciplined army of revolutionaries—not a chaotic
electorate—was necessary. Mobilization, essentially a military
concept, meant to Lenin that the revolutionary party would engage
in military-like activity. Lenin paid considerable attention to the
writings of military theorists, particularly Clausewitz's *On War*.
Engels's studies of the military demonstrate that he, too, possessed
a deep interest in the subject, especially regarding the German,

2. Selznick, *The Organizational Weapon*, pp. 1–2.

British, and French armies. Trotsky also was a student of the military. To the pragmatic Marxists, the immediate and manifest foe was the traditional professional army, viewed as the nationalist instrument of the capitalist state. At the same time, they were fascinated by it, and eventually patterned the Soviet army after it, despite the nostalgic preference of Trotsky and others for the Paris Commune model.

The Bolshevik party was an effective organizational weapon because it solved many of the problems associated with transforming a voluntary association into a managerial structure. But once a strong structure was in place and ideology had become merely an adjunct, the party became obsessive in exploiting opportunities to conquer social institutions.

Translated into reality, the dictatorship of the proletariat led to formation of the first party-state in modern history. The dictatorship of the proletariat had multiple targets; it sought to liquidate czarist power, political parties, parliament, and internal party opposition. It was designed to mobilize the masses from above and to direct the revolution according to Marxist-Leninist principles. Political support would grow from the party's vanguard—the professional revolutionaries—teaching the toiling masses their new role: an organized, state-dominated People. For that purpose the party became an *apparat*—a machine for revolutionary purposes—and its workers apparatchiks. The party was to be the vanguard, and it would not tolerate the leader following the masses (Khvostism) because Lenin identified that arrangement with bourgeois socialism.

The soviets' councils of workers and peasants in factories, cities, and rural centers were designed to conquer the state, liquidate czarism, and establish a transitional political system that would be directed, staffed, and dominated by the party. When Lenin called for the 1917 revolution, his battle cry was "all power to the soviets," and these councils did successfully mobilize political power and create the Soviet state by fiat. Subsequently, the concept of the soviet became the basis for the Soviet Union's first governmental structure.

Parallel Structures. After czarist institutions and the infant party and parliamentary structures had been annihilated, Lenin set about to establish the party's supremacy. Because the party had provided the impetus for the mobilization, legitimization, and consolidation of bolshevik power, its chief structures became the supreme organs of the state. Lenin created two new pyramids of power that paralleled the historical organization of local and state government and of national authority, and which remain intact. One, based on the village and town soviets, feeds into the district soviets and congresses for regions and republics, which converge in the All Union Congress of Soviets.[3] The soviets, which have both legislative and executive functions, replaced the czarist autocracy without adopting the Western parliamentary system. The other power pyramid is the party executive, which holds political monopoly over the state.[4] An exclusionary body in the Soviet Union's power structure, the Politburo began as a collective enterprise in which Lenin was first among equals and grew into a tyranny under Stalin. Today, it is a coalition of managers, apparatchiks, technocrats, militarists, and ideologues. Nevertheless, the party continues to resemble a pyramid erected on a territorial and functional foundation.[5]

The party dominates the soviet-based structure and appoints its leaders. The original ambiguity of party-soviet relations in 1917 has been eliminated, the state functions are demarcated clearly, and the party repeatedly and unequivocally asserts it supremacy. "The Party leads the Soviets," wrote Stalin in *Problems of Leninism*.[6] The dictatorship of the proletariat, now alternately called the Politburo, or the Presidium, leads the party.

Although Lenin's party-state became the model for all communist authoritarian regimes, modifications are common. In China, for instance, the symbiotic relationship between the party and the army has given the latter more importance in the highest political organs than the Soviet army enjoys.[7] Nevertheless, the

3. *Encyclopedia of the Social Sciences* (1934), s.v. "Soviets."
4. Towster, *Political Power in the USSR*, pp. 119–83, is still a useful analysis of party-Soviet relationships. See also Fainsod, *How Russia Is Ruled*, pp. 209–45.
5. Towster, *Political Power in the USSR*, p. 135.
6. Ibid., pp. 179–80.
7. On China, see Franz Schurmann, *Ideology and Organization in Communist China* (Berkeley: University of California Press, 1966); Benjamin Schwartz, *Chinese Communism and the Rise of Mao* (Cambridge: Mass.: Harvard University Press, 1953); William Whitson, *The Chinese High*

principle that the party parallels the structures of the state and
that the two are linked is as firm in China as in such modern authoritarian bolshevik states as East Germany, Rumania, and
Czechoslovakia. Analysis of bolshevik political behavior must focus
on the party's internal power struggles, its composition, and its
changing functions. It must also consider the party-state struggle
at many different levels and the rivalry between and within the
organs of the party-state. The politics of Soviet authoritarianism
are those of the most complex system of parallel structures in the
world.

Auxiliary Structures. Although the paramount party-state system
inherently diminishes its auxiliary structures, they have some influence. Unlike the nazi and fascist paramilitary organizations,
however, the bolshevik auxiliary political instruments are not autonomous. The political police and the youth movement are party-
state organs and therefore are subordinate politically and
functionally. In all of its manifestations, from NKVD to KGB, from
Dzerzinsky to Shelepin, the political police—the regime's instrument of terror—has been both an internal and external security
system.[8] Its primary function has always been to defend the party's
political monopoly; defense of the state is a secondary concern. The
police protect the dominant institutions and their rulers and,
under Stalin's dictatorship, served as an espionage agency and terror machine in both party and state. Although control over the
economy, the state, and the soviets may have relaxed somewhat in
recent years, in regulating ideas and culture, the political police
are at least as effective now as when they were established in 1917.

The political police are the clearest manifestation of the tyrannical and despotic aspects of Soviet authoritarianism. There were
times during the Great Terror when the police dominated the

Command (New York: Praeger, 1972); Ellis Joffe, *Party and Army Professionalism and Political Control of the Chinese Officer Corps, 1949–1964*
(Cambridge, Mass.: Harvard University Press, East Asian Monographs,
1965); and Amos Perlmutter, *The Military and Politics in Modern Times*
(New Haven: Yale University Press, 1977).

8. On the Soviet police, see Fainsod, *How Russia Is Ruled*, pp. 421–62.

party.[9] Although their influence has decreased since Stalin and Beria died, the political police are nevertheless a major agency available to the party to defend its monopoly against political and ideological rivals. Although the police ostensibly protect the party, its members have by no means been sacrosanct; in fact, the most prominent victims of the police have been party luminaries.

The Komsomol—the bolshevik youth movement—plays an important ideological and socializing function for the party. It too is designed to enhance the party's reputation and to secure its longevity.

The Nazi Model

Contrary to the claims of the totalitarian school of Arendt and Friedrich and the "fascist epoch" school of Nolte, to a small degree the Nazi party did serve as a model for other parties and systems just as the Bolshevik party did. Moreover, it was not totalitarian in the functional sense, but only in the metapolitical sense.

Anyone acquainted with the abundant literature on the subject can have no doubts that the Nazi party's rise to power between 1919 and 1933 and its major successes were due to the führer's leadership, propaganda, and superior organization.[10] In fact, after the Beer Hall Putsch of 1923, Hitler decided to abandon the insurrectionist approach to politics. Once he was released from prison in

9. On the Soviet terror machine, see the seminal work of Robert Conquest, *The Great Terror* (New York: Macmillian, 1968); Aleksandr Solzhenitsyn, *The Gulag Archipelago 1918–1956*, 3 vols. (New York: Harper and Row, 1974, 1975, 1976); and Zbigniew Brzezinski, *The Permanent Purge* (Cambridge, Mass.: Harvard University Press, 1955).

10. On Nazi party organization and mobilization before 1933, see Dietrich Orlow, *The History of the Nazi Party, 1919–1933* (Pittsburgh: University of Pittsburgh Press, 1969); Karl Bracher, *The German Dictatorship* (New York: Praeger, 1970); Bracher, Sauer and Schultz, *Die Nationalsozialistische Machtergreifung*, 2d ed. (Cologne-Opladen: Westdeutscher Verlag, 1962); J. Noakes and G. Pridham, eds., *Documents on Nazism: 1919–1945* (New York: Viking Press, 1974); Wolfgang Sauer, "National Socialism: Totalitarianism or Fascism?" *American Historical Review* 73 (1966), pp. 404–24; and Geoffrey Pridham, *Hitler's Rise to Power* (New York: Harper Torchbooks, 1973).

1925, Hitler took a traditional path and engaged in parliamentary politics. Nevertheless, both before and after its 1933 electoral victory, the Nazi party was no ordinary party. It distinguished itself in three areas: its mobilization of the electorate; its propaganda machinery; and its auxiliary instruments, including youth squads, the militia, the SA, and the SS.

Political Support. Although predominantly a middle-class organization in membership and electoral support, the appeal of the Nazi party was universal.[11] Between 1929 and 1933, it became one of Germany's mass movements, creating a constituency more broadly based than that of either the Communist or the Social Democratic party.[12] Both propaganda and organization contributed to its electoral success, but social and economic unrest also created new party members. Between 1919 and 1923, the Nazi party competed for them against three hundred assorted patriotic militias, nationalist and socialist coteries, and parties in Germany.[13]

After the abortive putsch, Hitler's imprisonment, and what amounted to the dissolution of the party, Hitler made his comeback with a small militant group, his "professional revolutionaries," the *Alte Kämpfer* ("old fighters"). Another group of professional Nazis was the "vanguard generation," mostly noncommissioned and junior officers who were veterans of the World War I. Still another group, the *völkisch* ideologues, were middle class in origin, and included anti-Semitic, nationalist teachers and professors, journalists, and the parvenu intelligentsia.[14] These three groups formed the nucleus of what became a formidable party or-

11. Orlow, *History of the Nazi Party, 1919–1933*, pp. 128–84; and Noakes and Pridham, *Documents on Nazism.*
12. Joachim Fest, *Hitler* (New York: Harcourt Brace, 1963), pp. 259–370; Pridham, *Hitler's Rise to Power*, pp. 184–94; J. Noakes, *The Nazi Party in Lower Saxony, 1921–1933* (Oxford: Oxford University Press, 1971), pp. 108–38; and Juan Linz, "Comparative Study of Fascism," in *Fascism*, ed. Walter Z. Laqueur (Berkeley: University of California Press, 1976), pp. 74–77.
13. Harold J. Gordon, *Hitler and the Beer Hall Putsch* (Princeton, N.J.: Princeton University Press, 1972), pp. 88–119. This is the most authoritative and comprehensive study of German patriotic societies.
14. Orlow, *History of the Nazi Party, 1919–1933*, pp. 46–53.

ganization. Although in its small size and purpose the group was similar to Lenin's original body of followers, the Nazi "pioneers" were primarily lower- and middle-class anti-Semites, while Lenin's party was composed largely of middle- and upper-class intellectuals. By 1929, Hitler was able to use the organization in a strategy that brought him to the chancellorship in 1933.

Not unlike a modern politician in a pluralistic democratic system, Hitler mapped an electoral strategy for Germany that skillfully played upon geography, class interests, and social cleavages to win votes. He sought to appeal to a wide range of constituents—from workers to industrialists, primitivistic rebels to upper-middle-class architects and even aristocrats. Hitler clearly understood the uses of money in elections and his political-financial advisor and party treasurer, Franz Xaver Schwarz, applied his wizardry to the rationalization of party administration and electoral organization. The Nazi party became a model of a modern political party: efficient, resilient, highly organized, and well financed. Combined with the dedicated Old Fighters, Veterans, and propagandists, and led by the charismatic Hitler, the Nazis were a modern authoritarian party.

Parallel and Auxiliary Structures. The most conspicuous political auxiliary structure under nazism was the propaganda machinery. Not a simple or regular bureaucracy, it played a key role in sustaining the Nazis in power. There is little argument that Hitler and his chief of propaganda, the ingenious Dr. Goebbels, played an extraordinary role in the development of thought control. Hitler was a master propagandist who had started his career in the propaganda branch of the Munich military in 1919, but unlike Lenin he did not establish the Nazi party as an agency for the education of the party cadres. This failure significantly affected its development and is one of the important ways in which the Nazi party differed conceptually from the Soviet Communist party. Before 1933, Hitler did not intend the Nazi party to exercise a political monopoly. The party was designed principally to win elections; therefore it used propaganda to capture the electorate by manipulating the themes of nationalism, the "Stab in the Back" at Versailles, the German unification question, and the Jews. Nazi propaganda appealed to

the basic, and basest, values of the German middle and lower middle classes, the workers, and the peasants as well as to the right
wing, the anti-Semitic intelligentsia, and the aristocrats. But
Goebbels' major political task was to build up Hitler's image and
document the need for the führer in postwar Germany. Nazi propaganda therefore was devised as a means of achieving electoral
power, not as a Soviet-style instrument of mind and thought control. The propaganda machinery was more of an auxiliary instrument than an integral component of the party or of the Nazi state.

What distinguished the Soviet system from its Nazi and Fascist
counterparts is that in the former, the parallel and auxiliary structures are crucial to the regime. In Nazi and Fascist regimes, personal dictatorship substituted for the need always to employ parallel structures.

The Fascist and Nazi regimes, once in power, did not establish
the party as a structure parallel to the state as in the USSR. They
certainly recruited the party elite into the highest positions of the
state, but, in the Nazi case, most of the upper and certainly the
middle class was not nazi, and the party's efforts to infiltrate the
army were not very successful. The higher institutions of the Nazi
party did not serve as a reservoir for the state bureaucracy. For
Hitler, however, it sufficed that the regime was nazi and that he
totally dominated the system. This he accomplished by relying on
auxiliary structures, especially the political and party police.

In contrast to the Soviet regime, the Fascist and Nazi regimes
evolved from radical nationalist coteries. Their ranks included unemployed veterans, members of youth movements, and romantic
poets. The Nazis possessed, in addition, a group of paranoid anti-
Semites, the *lumpen* intellectuals and *unterwelt* "philosophers."
Gordon's description of the Nazi party and their like is perhaps the
most accurate:

> The Patriotic Bands were basically political paramilitary or-
> ganizations, although some of them had purely civilian branches,
> and theoretically were some of the most important. . . . In
> fact, however, the significance of all of them, aside from the
> NSDAP, lay predominantly in their military potential. It was
> their military coloration that gave them character and it was

their military organization and arms that gave them a political weight well beyond that which their numbers alone would have brought.[15]

The Nazis occupied the same position in the German Patriotic Movement that the Communist party occupied in the Marxist movement.[16] They were the most vigorous party in the movement and, once Hitler assumed control, they developed superior organizational and propaganda machineries. Like the Bolsheviks before 1917, the Nazi party before 1923 was insurrectionist and revolutionary—an instrument of violence. Its paramilitary organization was a fundamental part of it. The Bolshevik party, on the other hand, did not develop a formal paramilitary structure, but its vanguard elite did the same job for them.

Auxiliary Structures: The Storm Troops and the Waffen SS. Between the wars, Germany spawned the most remarkable paramilitary movement in modern history.[17] These organizations, which com-

15. Gordon, *Hitler and the Beer Hall Putsch*, p. 88.
16. Ibid., p. 49.
17. The literature on private and political armies and elite fascist and Nazi groups and youth movements is proliferating. George L. Mosse, *Crisis in German Ideology* (New York: Grosset and Dunlap, 1963), is a penetrating study of the myth and of German volkish movements and orientations. Walter Z. Laqueur, *Young Germany* (New York: Basic Books, 1962), is another. The analysis in Robert G. L. Waite, *Vanguard of Nazism* (Cambridge, Mass.: Harvard University Press, 1952) is one of the best on private armies. George H. Stein, *The Waffen SS, 1939–1945* (Ithaca, N.Y.: Cornell University Press, 1966), is a thorough analysis with some extraordinarily broad conclusions on the subject. Heinz Hohne, *The Order of the Death's Head* (New York: Coward-McCann, 1969), is a competent journalistic and documentary account of that macabre elite. Bracher, *The German Dictatorship*, the leading study of Hitler's Germany, includes penetrating conclusions on the Nazi youth movement, ideology, and symbolism. Hans Buchheim, *SS und Polizei im NS Statt* (Bonn: Selbstervlag der Studiengeselleschaft für Zeitproblem, 1964), is a thorough account. A superior study of the SS in Helmut Krausnick et al., eds., *Anatomy of the SS State* (New York: Walker, 1966). Both Waite and Hohne contain highly selective bibliographies on the SS. On the struggle between the SS and the Reichswehr and Hitler's role in it, see Hans Buchheim, "The Position of the SS in the Third Reich," in *Republic to Reich*, ed. Hajo Holborn (New York: Pantheon Books, 1972), pp. 251–97.

bined youth, idealism, nationalism, and violence, were motivated by zealotry and buttressed by elitist practices. Violent marches, vandalism, and killing were widespread. Between the era of the Free Corps (1918) and that of the Waffen SS (1941), these paramilitary organizations, some of them autonomous, were so numerous that they defy cataloging here. The SS, the SA, the Waffen SS, the Allgemeine SS, the Steinwerke, Himmler's system RSHA, the Gestapo, the Schutzpolizei, and others shared a common dedication to rightist revolutionary activities. They used political violence, assassination, and paramilitary action to police and silence liberals, socialists, and democrats. One of Hitler's most remarkable achievements was to harness and subjugate them to the Nazi state and military apparatus by professionalizing the nationalist romantic revolutionaries who composed them.

A movement that appeals to the romantic revolutionary soldier exhibits definite ideological and organizational characteristics. Ideologically, it resembles a *jugend kultur*, a youth movement, which is antibourgeois, antidemocratic, antiliberal, and fascist. It is also chauvinist, extremist, nostalgic, and romantic. Dedication to war is a personal and group aspiration. "War," writes Ernst Junger, "the Father of all things, is also our father.... What we wanted was war and adventure, excitement and destruction." Violence is considered an act of personal and national liberation. To crush the left, especially leftist revolts, is an overwhelming need. Activism and nihilism are viewed as the proper attitudes toward an established order. "What do we believe in, you ask," Junger writes. "Nothing besides the possibility of action."

On the organizational level, such movements were led by a well-trained, cohesive elite supported by a system of youth auxiliaries. "Storm" abilities and fierce cloak and dagger skills were developed and maintained. There was strict "to the death" (*Kadaver*) discipline. Though hierarchical, such societies were egalitarian and classless. The familiar *du* was used, and there was a large number of noncommissioned officers, some of whom even served as battalion commanders. Spartan, emphasizing excellent physical condition, the societies kept membership secret and strictly voluntary. They operated clandestinely.[18]

18. Stein, *The Waffen SS*, pp. 282, 284.

In the seamy world of the Munich Patriotic Movement's defense leagues, the most notorious figure was a war veteran and former captain, Ernst Roehm. Roehm's prominence was the result of his influential connections and the simplicity of his ideas.[19] He was a true rightist revolutionary who believed in establishing Hitler's version of national socialism by means of a paramilitary organization that eventually would achieve political power by violent means. This was the origin of the SA—the Storm Troopers. Roehm advocated a sustained revolution: the permanent march of the German masses into history, following the tradition of the Freikorps, which Waite called the "vanguard" of Nazism.[20]

Roehm's SA was to become an autonomous mass organization that lent "military" support to the Nazi party when Roehm deemed it necessary. However, when Hitler began to rebuild the party in 1925 he envisioned for and ultimately imposed on the SA a different role "as a body of political agitators and fighters absolutely subordinate to the party."[21]

When Roehm abandoned the SA leadership in 1925 and departed for Bolivia, Hitler decided that the SA should become a staff guard. Another personal bodyguard eventually became known as the SS. By 1933, when Hitler became chancellor, the SA was a mass movement of 250,000—400,000 in 1934—which provided a great scope for maneuver on the part of the recently returned Ernst Roehm. Roehm's concept of the mass movement was diametrically opposed to Himmler's concept of the elite. The result was the revolt of Roehm's SA in June 1934. The uprising, which was not aimed against Hitler, was finally quelled by Hitler, his SS henchmen, and the Reichswehr officers, all of whom were apprehensive about the SA's monopoly over legitimized state violence.

During the march to power, Roehm threatened the Nazi party but not Hitler. Not only did he command a formidable paramilitary organization but he represented the quintessence of the Nazi revolution. His destruction and the subordination of the SA was necessary in order for Hitler to consolidate his power. Yet even the

19. Herman Mau, "The 'Second Revolution'—June 30, 1934" in *Republic to Reich*, ed. Hajo Holborn (New York: Pantheon Books, 1972).

20. Waite, *Vanguard of Nazism*. See also Perlmutter, *Military and Politics in Modern Times*.

21. Buchheim, "The Position of the SS," p. 253.

"sacrifice" of Roehm's macabre, armed romantics in the name of
stability was not sufficient. Hitler needed more than a party bodyguard; he needed a private army. In this capacity, the SS
Blackshirts served him well.[22]

In Germany, the emergence of the SS marked the change from
anarchy to nazi order. The SS was distinguished from the Storm
Troopers by its subservience solely to Hitler; it eventually became
a professional, elitist military group. It was Hitler's praetorian
guard and his pride during the war. By 1936, the armed SS had
been divided into two services with clearly defined roles and
functions: the SS Verfugungstruppe, or Hitler's bodyguard, which
eventually became the military SS or Waffen SS, and the SS To-
tenkopfverbande, heir to the Storm Troopers. The SS Toten-
kopfverbande was an organization composed of bullies and sadists.
It was in charge of police activities and the concentration camps
that were part of the final solution for Jews and other despised
peoples. Both SS revolutionary armies were legitimized as "organizations in the service of the state" only because they served the
dictator himself.

"Indeed," writes George Stein, "it was the SS, not the National
Socialist Party, that proved to be the dynamic core of the Nazi system." But its loyalty was to the dictator, not the state. The Waffen
SS took the following oath: "I swear to you, Adolf Hitler, as Führer
and Reichschancellor, loyalty and bravery. I vow to you, and those
you have named to command me, obedience unto death, so help me
God." Like all revolutionary armies, it was task-oriented. It was
intended to serve as Hitler's elite guard during the transition
period, which would probably last through the war. It was designed to protect the führer and his regime by acting as a
militarized police force. Hitler (unlike Himmler) never intended
the SS to become an established military institution.

Hitler's decision to allow the armed SS to take an active part in
the war was based on his conviction that it would not be able to

22. On the struggle between the SS and the Reichswehr and the com-
plicity of the SS in the dismissal of the tow field marshals in 1938, see
Harold Deutsch, *Hitler and His Generals* (Minneapolis: University of Minnesota Press, 1974); and Robert O'Neill, *The German Army and the Nazi
Party: 1919–1939* (London: Macmillan, 1953), pp. 333–455.

retain the respect of Germans unless it did its share at the front. Hitler regarded the Waffen SS in its military role as a Guard formation, in the eighteenth- and nineteenth-century meaning of the term. As the military apotheosis of National Socialism, its task was to set an example for the Army.[23]

If the Nazi Party aspired to be the vanguard of the "German race," the SS sought a revolutionary role in leading the German military establishment. Although the Waffen SS fought valiantly and achieved a considerable military reputation on the Eastern front, it was never accepted by the Wehrmacht as a legitimate military organization. Beginning as an instrument of terror, the organization of revolutionary soldiers became an appendage of the state war machine and failed to achieve legitimacy based on its own merits. It never became institutionalized as part of the regular military establishment; its function was revolutionary action, and because it was imbued with the Nazi *geist* ("spirit"), it served as the vanguard of the revolutionary party.

Hitler himself clearly distinguished between the functions of the revolutionary and those of the professional soldier. "He had no intention of creating a fourth branch of the Wehrmacht," which was "the spearhead of Nazi aggression."[24] The Waffen SS was the heir to the Free Corps. "Few of the men in the Waffen SS were old enough to have had any personal contact with the post–World War I Freikorps movement; yet it was the spirit of their movement, its nihilism and elitism, which perhaps comes closest to that of the Waffen SS."[25] Both organizations were distinguished from the established military force by their emphasis on toughness, recklessness, and savagery at the expense of skill, training, order, and military education. They acquired the spirit which made them ruthless from such abandon. The egalitarianism and cohesion of the Freikorps were emulated; even its military uniform was adopted. The heroes of the SS troops were not the brutal police, the Alte Kämpfer of Hitler's early days, but regular army offers who had commanded the SS Verfügungstruppe. The Waffen SS shared the

23. Stein, *The Waffen SS*, pp. 282–83.
24. Ibid.
25. Quoted in Perlmutter, *The Military and Politics in Modern Times*, p. 215.

egalitarianism, as well as the high political commitment, of all modern revolutionary soldiers.

As Hitler's private army, the SS became one of two parallel instruments of the dual state,[26] a term that describes Germany after 1940. On the one side was the führer's despotic authority, bolstered by the SS, and on the other was the Gauleiter (Nazi district leaders) who tried to dominate, not always successfully, the administrative machinery of the *Gleichschaltung* Nazi state.[27] Gleichschaltung policy was an effort to dominate interest groups and classes and bring them into line with the party by the creation of "a massive, centralized corps of staff officials at all levels of the party's vertical organization who developed plans (at the top) and carried on propaganda (at all levels) designed to appeal to a specific social or economic group."[28] This was one of the chief functions of the dual state: to politicize and nazify class and group interests. The Nazis successfully applied Gleichschaltung policy to farmers, artisans, and small shopkeepers. As we shall see later, they were not successful with either the civil service or the military.

The SS thus became Hitler's chief instrument of domination. It played a crucial role in annihilating the SA, it intervened in the affairs of the Reichswehr's high command, and it was instrumental in the dismissal of Field Marshals Von Fritsch and Von Blomberg in 1938.[29] The SS also infiltrated the police. By 1940, the Reichsführer of the SS, Heinrich Himmler, fulfilled a personal dream when he became chief of the state police. The political police were now merged with state police, blurring the functional parallelism between the two and establishing a unified police state.

This achievement must be contrasted with the Bolshevik experience, in which the political police were either party instruments or subordinates of the party-state (as were all other parallel

26. On the concept of the dual state, see Ernst Fraenkel, *The Dual State: A Contribution to the Theory of Dictatorship* (New York: Oxford University Press, 1941).

27. See Bracher, *The German Dictatorship*, pp. 247–48 for a discussion of the Gleichschaltung policy.

28. Ibid., p. 235.

29. See William S. Allen, *The Nazi Seizure of Power* (Chicago: Quadrangle, 1965).

and auxiliary structures). While the Bolshevik party strove for political monopoly over the state, the party in Germany was not as imposing as the Nazi state and the regime's goal became simply to defend Hitler's tyranny.

The SS linked the Nazi state and party to Hitler. Thus, despotism, charisma, and a praetorian political police maintained the Nazi state, and the party, the führer, and the SS dominated it. Nazi authoritarianism more resembled classical tyranny than totalitarianism. What differentiates nazism from classical tyrannies, however, is the existence of a police state, a new type of modern authoritarian regime.

The Nazi regime certainly was *not* a party-state system. Not only were the relationships between the party and the state unequal, but while the Soviets inherited a weak state and political chaos, the Nazis came to power in a country with a relatively stable state. While the Bolshevik apparatus was a new type of party, the Nazi party apparatus could be included in Sigmund Neumann's ideal of *Weltanschauung* ("world view") parties, which comprised Social and Christian Democratic parties. The Nazi party still depended on the traditional state bureaucracy, and it only slowly, and incompletely, Nazified the state. The bolshevik state was 'Sovietized' from its very inception.[30] On the whole, the Nazi state was a traditional one. Unlike the Bolshevik party, the Nazi party did not employ the state to integrate the society. The Nazi state and party were not as symbiotic as the Bolshevik party and state always have been. The party never became the people's community that Robert Ley, the Nazi minister of labor wanted it to become.[31] As a *Weltanschauungen* party, it was more closely related to German society and was certainly more popular than the Soviet party, but it never became integrated into the state.

The concepts of the professional revolutionary and the party elite did not exist in the Nazi party. The Nazi party elite was a

30. Although Dietrich Orlow speaks of the "partyfication"—an awkward term for *partinost* or *Parteilichkeit*—of the German society, even the Gleichschaltung state was not nazified. See Dietrich Orlow, *The History of the Nazi Party, 1933–1945* (Pittsburgh: University of Pittsburgh Press, 1973), pp. 3–17.

31. Ibid., p. 15.

concentric group surrounding the führer—"an access to Hitler group"—dependent on Hitler's charisma, not on the bureaucratic and hierarchical system of party leadership that so clearly characterizes the Bolsheviks.[32] The Nazi elite, again unlike the Soviets, did not derive its power from ideological commitments, but from loyalty to Hitler. The distinction between party and state was clear-cut in Nazi Germany even if some Nazi leaders held party and state jobs simultaneously.[33] But while the Bolshevik party created the Soviet state and the lines of demarcation between the two became blurred over time, the Nazi party-state rivalry was notorious. Although senior bureaucrats joined the party, voluntarily or otherwise, they (except for opportunists and sycophants) considered themselves a class of their own; as enlightened figures, they were contemptuous of the relatively uneducated Nazi slobs. This could hardly be said of the relationship between party and state in the USSR.

To reiterate, the Nazi party was not an "organizational weapon" to penetrate society and the state—this, in fact, was the Bolshevik trademark. The Nazi Party was a *Weltanschauungen* authoritarian party dominated by Hitler's charismatic leadership. Relationships within the party elite were not ideological but personalist. Outwardly, the party's organizational structures made it look like the facade of a totalitarian party—for example, the Bolshevik party-state. The Nazis were elitist, even if their aspirations were populist,[34] but the regime was not a Bolshevik *partinost* ("partyism"). According to Orlow, "The NSDAP's *Weltanschauung* was rudimentary in comparison to the far more developed ideologies of the totalitarian parties derived from a Marxist base."[35] The party did not opt for a welfare role. On the contrary, the bureaucratic concept of Hess, Bormann, and Schwarz prevailed, but it was totally dependent on the führer. Cadres, agitation, and *Edinonchelo* (leadership) were not the aspirations of the Nazi party leaders, and these concepts were "Prussianized" as their influence declined. Though they tried hard, the Nazis could

32. Ibid., pp. 7–8.
33. Ibid.
34. Ibid., pp. 15–17.
35. Ibid., p. 14.

not destroy the Prussian state bureaucracy and military and left the Nazi state composed of nonmovement groups, elites, and structures. All nonmovement elements were destroyed in the USSR. As noted earlier, propaganda is not the same as agitation. Nazi party leaders did not even consider a Bolshevik party organizational setup. The Nazi party was not established to create a new society or to engage in social and economic experimentation, but to enhance the German race. The Nazis were classical state capitalists and were antiliberal, anticonservative and antibourgeois in orientation and in practice. They were radical nationalists, not creators of a new type of society. It is the different nature, structure, and aspirations, as well as the dynamics, of bolshevist Leninism that gave the Soviet party a different tone and character and led to the modern party-state authoritarian model.

The Fascist Model

Fascism is a political, intellectual, and ideological movement that, according to Renzo De Felice, is rigidly restricted. "It must be limited chronologically, between the two wars. It must be limited, geographically, to Western Europe, that part of Europe that had undergone a process of liberalization and democratization. Finally, it must be limited from a social point of view. *Fascism, in its emergence and affirmation, is a phenomenon of the middle classes"*[36] (italics mine).

The fascist movement was the first to espouse a modern authoritarian credo—an antiliberal, antidemocratic, antibourgeois, and revisionist Marxist ideology inspired by national syndicalism. The emergence of fascism in Italy accompanied the growth of similar authoritarian movements in almost all of the former territories of the Austro-Hungarian Empire, including Hungary and Rumania. (Czechoslovakia, until 1939, was the exception, although native fascism was present even there.) In these countries, fascist movements grew fast, and fascist regimes emerged in eastern and southeastern Europe. The most notorious were Archangel Michael

36. Renzo De Felice, *The Interpretations of Fascism* (Cambridge, Mass.: Harvard University Press, 1977), pp. 89–90.

in Rumania and the Arrow Cross in Hungary. In southern Europe, including Spain and Portugal, the movements were corporate authoritarian in nature. Authoritarianism and modern oligarchic praetorianism eventually developed as well in the British-French Mandate provinces of the fallen Ottoman Empire. In Arab areas in the 1930s and 1940s, fascist movements linked to nationalist parties continued to thrive, especially in Iraq, Syria, Lebanon, and Egypt, but except in Egypt they lost power to the authoritarian praetorian regimes.

In Italy, the fascist movement was an ideological mixture of syndicalism and corporatism. Fascism, which is a much maligned concept, was born in ambiguity and is subject to highly disparate and controversial interpretations.[37] As discussed earlier, it was the outcome of the crisis of classical Marxism, influenced by Italian politics and society and, above all, by revolutionary and nationalist syndicalism.[38] A mass-mobilizing, developmental authoritarian movement, it is, to reiterate Gregor, a heretical form of Marxism. It is syndicalism in its proletarian-nationalist phase.

Gregor conclusively demonstrates the linkage between syndicalism, nationalism, economic developmentalism, and fascism. In fact, Mussolini and his chief ideologues believed that the intellectual sources of fascism were Marxism, syndicalism, and nationalism.[39] Analyzing the theoretical formulations of its chief ideologues—Mussolini, Olivetti, Bottai, Panunzio, Rocco, and Gentile—Gregor illustrates the trend that led from heretical Marxism via syndicalism to national socialism, that is, fascism. The essential antibourgeois, anticlerical orientations of fascism were derived from syndicalism, but fascism discarded its antistate and

37. De Felice, *The Interpretations of Fascism;* A. James Gregor, *Interpretations of Fascism* (New Jersey: General Learning Press, 1974).

38. I am most grateful to A. James Gregor, whose instruction led me to revise my thoughts about fascism. Most of what follows has been inspired and directly influenced by his writings. I single out his lastest work, which this discussion follows very closely: *Italian Fascism and Developmental Dictatorship* (Princeton, N.J.: Prenceton University Press, 1979). See also A. James Gregor, *Survey of Marxism* (New York: Random House, 1965); and A. James Gregor, *The Fascist Persuasion in Radical Politics* (Princeton, N.J.: Princeton University Press, 1974).

39. Gregor, *Italian Fascism and Developmental Dictatorship*, pp. 64–126.

antimilitaristic elements.[40] Some Syndicalists became militants in the trenches of the First World War; the war experience and patriotic propaganda were powerful influences on them. Patriotism became synonomous with "progressivism," that is, with the revolutionary Italian syndicalists' struggle against the reactionary Ottoman Empire, which led to the Italo-Ottoman War of 1912. As De Felice wrote elsewhere, fascism was a creature of the First World War.[41]

The corporate concepts that emerged in those years— syndicates and economic associations—originated with Panunzio, the syndicalist-nationalist theoretician.[42] Unquestionably, the transformation of Syndicalist into Fascists was marked by the former's move away from Marxism and nationalist and revolutionary slogans to an elaborate doctrine based on economic developmentalism. The number of economists, sociologists, and engineers among the Syndicalists was high; they united to devise this century's first developmental program. Gregor shows that there is little doubt that the 1919 fascist program of San Sepolcro insisted on the need for Italian regeneration and advocated "a vast program of economic and political modernization and development."[43] The rapid expansion of production became central to the fascist economic program and was linked with national economic development. Fascist labor policy, which will be discussed later, demonstrated the mobilizational and participatory orientations of national syndicalism and fascism. After 1921, fascism became a mass movement.

Political Support and Mobilization. Initially, fascism was not a mass movement; instead, it appealed to an elite group of ex-servicemen, the *arditi* ("shock troops"), and officer volunteers.[44] Inspired by D'Annunzio's romantic millenarianism, fascism was

40. Ibid., pp. 64–73.
41. Gregor, *Italian Fascism*, pp. 73–83; and De Felice, *Interpretations of Fascism*.
42. Gregor, *Italian Fascism and Developmental Dictatorship*, pp. 83–85.
43. Ibid., pp. 101–11.
44. Adrian Lyttleton, *The Seizure of Power: Fascism in Italy, 1919–1939* (New York: Scribner's, 1972).

born as an antiparty, and as such it attracted futurists, poets, painters, radical nationalists, and a motley assortment of intellectuals and bohémes.

Early fascist ideology was essentially a call for action: it sought to awaken the spirit of the "dynamic minority." Like the Freikorps and the SA, the Italian fascists were young, idealistic, and militaristic. Their political orientations were as simplistic as Roehm's, consisting basically of marching from one piazza to another in an attempt to gain power through violence. The first nucleus was the paramilitary squadristi, who, like the SA, were anti-Bolshevik and combative. In fact, their name, *fasci di combattimento* ("bundle or band of fighters"), reveals much of their orientation. Fascism was not conceived as a party or a mobilizing structure, but as a spontaneous regional and urban conglomeration.

Fascism expanded during the 1920–21 period in both urban and rural areas, as the successful use of violence brought popularity.[45] Action produced more action, and unemployed veterans and malcontents joined in. In the provinces, the movement also attracted students and ex-servicemen. In Bologna, for instance, it thrived. In the capital of the rich agricultural region of Emilia-Romagna,[46] they succeeded in defeating the Socialists. In Milan, the movement was middle class in composition; in Genoa, it was petit bourgeois. The movement was not cohesive; its direction was unclear and its organization incoherent. The only thing which it was sure of was who its enemies were: the liberal state and the corruption and parliamentary chicanery typified by Giolitti.

Preparing for the 1921 election, the Fascist leaders, especially Mussolini, Grandi, and Balbo, began to move toward organizing the fasci into a political party. They encountered serious opposition because the squadristi and the D'Annunziani loved their freedom and were aghast at the prospect of entering parliamentary electoral politics. The predominant issue was the nature of politics, and Mussolini's new-found support for a republican tendency was not immediately duplicated by his provincial followers, many of whom were monarchists.[47]

45. Ibid., pp. 54–57.
46. Ibid., p. 57.
47. Ibid., p. 72.

Although it was not backed by any national consensus, a Fascist party was established in 1921. Mussolini began by seeking the cooperation of the industrialists and supporting any antisocialist laws that were enacted. He started to mobilize support with the planning of the March on Rome, which was intended to pit the squads against the Socialists and to intimidate government officials. But the underlying purpose was to defeat the Liberals and weaken parliament and the monarchy. Mussolini received support in this effort from the disgruntled urban middle class. The March on Rome, a classic D'Annunzian amorphous movement, was the beginning of the Fascist party.

The Fascist party never became a dominant political institution. The power of regional and local fascists in the provinces was greater than the party's national authority. Moreover, on the national level, the state undermined the party. Mussolini never succeeded in taming the party because he preferred to devote his attention to the conquest of the state.

Parallel and Auxiliary Instruments. In 1921, Mussolini inaugurated the Fascist Grand Council in an effort to establish a party executive that would parallel the state. This act strengthened Mussolini's personal position, but it did not restore party unity or pacify provincials who wanted military, rather than civilian, prefects and police chiefs.[48]

The major reasons for the party's inability to establish parallel institutions to dominate the state was clearly explained by a leading Fascist. "The state is not yet entirely in the hands of the Fascists because, as there are few men in our party to hold important offices, it is necessary to await the appearance of new technical and intellectual talent."[49] When aggressive fascism was transformed into a tranquil official cult and became bureaucratized and subordinated to the state, the revolutionary and so-called totalitarian phase of the movement came to an end. Mussolini opted to establish a corporate state paralleling the bureaucratic state, a strategy not known in Nazi Germany; his syndicalism led him to favor state

48. Ibid., pp. 164–65.
49. Ibid., p. 165.

incorporation of economic groups and interests. The state, which was the domain of the industrialists and unionists, was Mussolini's primary source of political support, since he was unable to rely on the party. His strategy was to become chief arbiter of the corporate state that was being formed under the cover of fascism. Corporatism soon afterward became synonymous with fascism.

The industrialists had considerable difficulty in accepting either the corporate state or fascism although their reluctance varied. The struggle between the sindicati and the fascist unions sometimes strengthened their position; in addition, Mussolini made considerable concessions to the industrialists, with whose support he could aggressively attack the extreme fascists. A political realist, Mussolini came to terms with some of the other historical enemies of fascism—the conservative military, the aristocracy, and, above all, the church. Although an avowed atheist, Mussolini knew the importance of Catholicism in Italy and adopted a policy of rapprochement with the church, even making Catholicism the state religion.

Many of Mussolini's actions—even his imperialistic adventures—were motivated by nationalist rather than fascist ideas. True Fascists like D'Annunzio wanted Italy to expand into Slavic eastern Europe and regain territories promised in the London Agreement. The direction of expansion favored by Mussolini— into the Eastern Mediterranean and Africa—was more along nationalist lines and was acceptable to traditional diplomats. Unlike a policy of expansion into eastern Europe, aggrandizement in this direction did not imply a radical position. Although Mussolini allegedly coined the word "totalitarianism," he directed a modern regime that was tyrannical and authoritarian, but not totalitarian.

Mussolini's corporatist offensive was not a fascist strategy, but a desperate effort to dominate the party and the state; it became his form of despotism and authoritarianism. He was not a Hitler who dominated the party and the state, not was he a Lenin or a Stalin, both of whom used the party against all opposing forces, including the state. Mussolini never relied exclusively on the Fascist party, its stalwarts, or its squadristi: he relied on the corporate state for political support. Nevertheless, as Lyttleton shows, his corporate offensive was short lived.[50] The party and the corporate state came to be at loggerheads and remained so until the end of the Fascist regime. The Fascists eventually turned to militarism, seeking to muster mass nationalist support through an aggressive foreign policy. Mussolini succeeded here; he aroused nationalism in a wide spectrum of Italians, including liberals, Catholics, fascists, and romantic D'Annunzians. Even more important was the relative prosperity and industrial peace that he brought to Italy.

Fascism was a mass mobilizing movement, regime, and party; its economic program was progressive, aggressive, and successful.[51] Rocco, the fascist ideologue, insisted on the creation of a national economic policy, state reform, and the reduction of dependency. Gregor meticulously reveals the influence that Michels, the sociologist who studied mass psychology, and the Italian elitist school of Mosca—especially Pareto—had on Fascism. Though Michels was not an early fascist ideologue, he joined the Fascist party after 1927 and was a member of the party school at Perugia. Michels called for mobilization of the masses. He thought that order could only be established through a leadership and an organization capable of psychological manipulation to energize the apathetic masses.[52] In the tradition of Mosca and Pareto, Michels was an elitist and called for the governance of the few over the many. Leadership must be aggressive but it also must possess organizational and manipulative skills. Here Michels resorted to the Sorelian dictum or to the role of the myth and "sentiments of nationality" to mobilize the nation.[53] But organization entails oligarchy. Oligarchy to sustain collectivity must be guided by a myth and a leader: "The leader became the incarnation of the nation."[54] It is a small step from this concept to fascist vanguardism. Thus elitism, vanguardism, and nationalist sentiments would transform

50. Ibid., pp. 312–13.
51. Gregor, *Italian Fascism and Developmental Dictatorship*, pp. 127–213.
52. Roberto Michels, *Political Parties* (Glencoe, Ill.: The Free Press, 1949). See also analysis of Michels in Gregor, *Italian Fascism and Developmental Dictatorship*, pp. 50–54, 218, 251–52, 268–74.
53. Gregor, *Italian Fascism and Developmental Dictatorship*, p. 242.
54. Ibid., p. 243.

the masses into action. The orchestration of a national consensus is the function of the fascist apparatus, propaganda, and ideology.

The manipulation of thought and ideas became an industry in Fascist Italy just as it always has been in the Bolshevik state. Radio and other mass media, education, and culture were all organized under the Fascist party umbrella, but fascist culture was the concern of the fascist regime, not of the party. In contradistinction to the party-state, the Fascist party did not become the educator of the nation; it was the nation's custodian and mobilizer. The task of thought reform and control was not assumed by the party.[55]

To reiterate, the most significant distinction that can be drawn between the Fascist, Nazi, and Bolshevik parties lies in their relationships to the state. The Bolshevik party had a paramount role in the monopolistic party-state. The boundaries between party and state in Nazi Germany were never clearly defined except in that Hitler's despotism was the only recognized authority; the SS and Nazi Gauleiter, who attempted to destroy the government of the Beamten (civil servants), the Heeresleitung (military high command), and the industrialists, were not very successful. In Fascist Italy, the state eventually superseded the party, and statism reigned supreme.

The Corporatist Model

Although it might seem that the corporatist model found in Spain, Portugal, and Latin America is an extension of the fascist type, it can be distinguished: corporatism, unlike fascism, is not a movement; the corporatist state, not the corporatist party, is the pillar of the system; the corporatist model begins and ends at the state and oligarchical levels; political mobilization is incidental and is mainly connected with serving the corporatist regime's need for legitimacy; the corporatist model makes no pretense to a collectivist ideology; like fascism, corporatism seeks to modernize the machinery of the society's economic structure; unlike fascism, cor-

---

55. I am grateful for these fine distinctions made in Lyttleton, *The Seizure of Power*, pp. 422–24.

poratism is a durable political and economic system found in the old and the new worlds.[56]

Corporatism Old and New. Corporatism should not be analytically restricted to Spain and Portugal, although they were the first to adopt the model after 1930; it is a West European phenomenon found in post–World War I Germany, Italy, and France. According to Charles Maier, it is the right's challenge to the left. It is an economic procedure designed to solve political problems outside of traditional political structures such as parliaments and political parties. Imbued with antiparliamentary and antiliberal ideas, consensus is sought not by appealing to the masses but through "continual bargaining among organized interests."[57] Organized groups, including the military, participate in national policy making and are able to exercise a political veto because the corporatist regime makes it costly for the government to resist the interests of these groups.[58] Political bargaining is conducted outside of parliament through government ministries and bureaucracies that are dominated by organized interest groups. The lines of distinction between society and state, parliament and the marketplace, and class and nation are dissolved.[59] Power becomes dependent on the state bureaucracy, and ministries that regulate economic and domestic

56. For the most informative political and social analysis of Franco's Spain, see Juan Linz, "An Authoritarian Regime: Spain," in *Mass Politics: Studies in Political Sociology,* ed. Eric Allard and Stein Rokkan (New York: Free Press, 1970), pp. 215–83; Juan Linz, "The Party System of Spain," in *Party Systems and Voter Alignments,* ed. S. M. Lipset and S. Rokkan (New York: Free Press, 1967), pp. 197–282; Juan Linz, "From Falange to Movimiento-Organización" in *Authoritarian Politics in Modern Societies,* ed. Samuel P. Huntington and Clement H. Moore, pp. 128–203; and Juan Linz, "The Future of an Authoritarian Situation," in *Authoritarian Brazil,* ed. Alfred Stepan (New Haven: Yale University Press, 1973), pp. 233–54. Because knowledge of authoritarianism in Portugal is meager, I will depend on the work of Wiarda, Linz, Schmitter, and several historians and will not generalize from the Portuguese case. Instead I will focus on the Spanish experience.

57. Charles Maier, *Recasting Bourgeois Europe* (Princeton, N.J.: Princeton University Press, 1975), p. 10. See pp. 3–19 for an analysis of corporatist Europe.

58. Ibid., p. 10.

59. Ibid.

affairs become the nerve centers of the corporatist state. Not unlike Mussolini's Fascist state, the corporatist state appeases the regular army and sometimes elevates the army into the central bureaucratic organization. It purchases the toleration of the directorial class.[60]

A short experiment with a corporatist state was the Vichy regime in France (1940–1944). In Vichy France, cartels—organized entities—were given a free hand and an official status. All levels of the economically active population—employers, managers, and workers—were organized into "natural" economic groupings which were functionally divided by branch, industry, and profession. They governed society and the economy autonomously but with direct protection from the state.[61]

According to Salazar, "The state has the right to foster, harmonize and control all national activities. . . . We wish to advance toward a new political economy, working in harmony with human nature, under the authority of a strong state which will protect the higher interests of the Nation, its wealth and its labor, both from capitalist excesses and from destructive Bolshevism."[62] Portugal's constitution of 1935 emphasized political control over moral behavior, which meant emulation of the traditional family and of the church. A clerical element was injected into the corporatist concept found in France and Italy although the state ensured "freedom of worship."[63] The church and the organized economic groups were recognized as corporatist and autonomous political units. In Portugal as elsewhere, the corporatist policy was not to irritate the army, the church, or vested economic interests.[64]

The Portuguese corporatist model was designed to weave an organic hierarchy composed of three layers of corporatist structures:

60. Ibid., pp. 556–57.

61. For a discussion of the corporatist state in Vichy, see Robert Paxton, *Vichy France: Old Guard and New Order: 1940–1944* (New York: Knopf, 1972), pp. 210–12.

62. From Salazar's speech to the Secretariat of National Propaganda, quoted in Charles F. Delzell, ed., *Mediterranean Fascism, 1919–1945, Selected Documents* (New York: Macmillan, 1970), p. 333.

63. For the 1933 constitution of Portugal, see Delzell, *Mediterranean Fascism*, pp. 338–46.

64. Ibid., p. 346.

primary (*sindicatos*), intermediary (union federation), and highest (corporations). On the top was an overarching structure called *copula* or the council of state. But the corporations did not come into existence until a quarter of a century after Salazar's takeover in 1933. Two auxiliary structures were initially established: economic coordination commissions and, more important, the collaborative agency—the party or *União Nacional*—that served to implement corporatism and its ideology. It was not a bolshevik party-state nor a fascist-nazi party; it was designed to serve as the regime's political instrument, the link of harmony between state and society.

Portugal is one modern state where a full-fledged corporatist regime was established.[65] Corporative institutions were also found in Austria, Poland, Italy, and France between 1919 and 1939 and in Brazil, Argentina, and Chile in the 1970s. Portugal is of particular interest because it demonstrates that there is no automatic linkage between corporatism and fascism, contrary to what some western historians and social scientists have argued.

Corporatism revived once again in Latin America as a Catholic solution to the problem of development and as an alternative to fascism, socialism and communism, with which it shares authoritarianism, collectivism, elitism, and exclusionism.[66] "An Iberic Latin counterpart to the modernizing ideologies of liberalism and socialism," corporate institutions serve "as agencies of controlled social change, with the emphasis on both the *control* and the *change*."[67] In Latin America and, especially, in Portugal, it is a pragmatic as well as an ideological and "natural" political course.

The corporate state of Salazar, Caetano, and Pereira strove to link individuals and society to the state. It represented a vertical hierarchy of social, religious, economic, and bureaucratic corporate structures that themselves were horizontally organized: the family, the church, the party, the bureacracy, the army, and the economic-functional corporatives from labor, industry, and ag-

65. Howard J. Wiarda, *Corporatism and Development: The Portuguese Experience* (Amherst: University of Massachusetts Press, 1977), p. 4.
66. Ibid., p. 63.
67. Ibid., p. 55.

riculture. The *Estado Novo* ("New State") was not a class-oriented state but a reflection of the traditional Roman and Medieval Catholic dualism between state religion and society.[68] It was basically an organic conception of the relationship between state and society. At the roots of corporative groups was the Roman and medieval system of guilds oriented toward harmony and social peace, as advocated by the Thomistic tradition, and led by the natural elites (*forus*) that guide the corporatist state.[69]

The corporatist state structure and political institutions extend their power to such corporate entities as the army (which plays a key role in Latin American states), the church, the guilds, and eventually to the *sindicatos*.[70] The corporatist intention is to overlay tradition and order with new ideas in order to meet changing circumstances, that is, to fuse traditional regard for order and hierarchy with the newer requirements of change and modernization.[71]

The Latin American political structure is designed to create and incorporate rising new socioeconomic sectors into the corporatist state system. Interest representation is replaced by a functional-organic hierarchy whose head is the corporatist state. Political structures of the corporatist state are authoritarian but not fascist. Mobilization is not aimed at individuals and it is not couched in radical ideologies. On the contrary, social mobilization is channeled through corporate entities, which are state controlled, while political participation is harnessed to the state through corporatist political structures, such as the church, army, and guilds.

The corporatist state, like the society under the party-state, seeks to secure the loyalty of the army. Unlike the party-state, however, it elevates the military to the role of *poder moderator* (arbiter) of the corporatist state. In the Salazar-Caetano state the army threatened the regime, which deterred intervention by appeasing it. This was also true of Franco's Spain. Legitimacy derived from membership in the corporatist hierarchy, where the army was sometimes equal to and at other times predominant over the church and the guilds. In contradistinction to Fascist Italy and

68. Ibid., pp. 55–89; a full analysis.
69. Ibid., p. 57.
70. Ibid., p. 61.
71. Ibid., p. 64.

some Eastern European regimes between the world wars, the corporatist state was conservative and antirevolutionary. It aspired to act as a stabilizing, harmonizing force, and it continues to do so in Latin America. It is not romantic, revolutionary, or class oriented. Nor is the corporatist state an integralist-Maurrasist, supernationalistic reaction to defeat, humiliation, and *dolchstosse* ("stab in the back"). It did not aspire, as did the Bolsheviks and Nazis, to establish the mass society. Once again, one should not confuse authoritarianism with totalitarianism. The party plays no role in the corporatist state, although it does in the economy. In some ways, it is an effort to resolve social and economic problems without resorting to politics; one could venture to say that there is no corporatist political theory.

Space does not permit an exhaustive analysis of Eastern European and Austrian corporate systems between 1919 and 1939. The Latin American system does have some elements in common with fascist movements such as that of pre-Franco Spain. One example is the birth of the Falange, which was a parallel and auxiliary instrument like the Freikorps and the squadristi in that it mixed social demagoguery with middle class values. It molded culture and values into a movement and party of poets, rovers, students, and terrorists.[72] In the beginning, it was not autonomous; inspired by an uneven mixture of Sorelian and Iberian syndicalism, nationalism, and nazi-fascist activism, it was led by José Antonio Primo de Rivera, an upper-middle-class son of a military officer.

The essential intellectual and political links between the Falange and Franco's single party were the nationalist, militarist, and syndicalist traditions. In essence, national syndicalism was antiliberal and Catholic. The Falange championed the "Patria," a transcendental unity guaranteed in a form of national coordination—an organic corporatist orientation. There was a nationwide syndicate system designed to guarantee economic justice and material production. José Antonio was no führer or duce, but he was the *jefe* ("boss") of the youth movement.[73] During the

72. The best study of the Falange is Stanley Payne's *Falange* (Stanford: Stanford University Press, 1962). Although the details of the Falange derive from Payne, the analysis is purely mine.
73. Ibid., pp. 38–58.

Spanish Civil War, the Falange had its own militia and was totally dedicated to increasing activism, but its contribution and effectiveness were slight.[74]

Like any dictator, Franco would not tolerate an autonomous group. By turning the Falange into the state party, he actually manipulated its ideology so that it would help to institutionalize his New Spain. The Falange then declined into an instrument of the right. It never became the instrument of the state its leaders hoped it would be, nor did it attain a position of political monopoly. Franco began his rule as the head of a strictly military junta (Junta de Defensa Nacional); it was this group that eventually institutionalized the dictatorship and harnessed the society through a state-dominated support party called the Movimiento-Organizacion. Even with a political arm, this monarchical-military regime was dominated totally by Franco, the caudillo.[75] Thus, in Spain, neither party nor state played the autonomous role that such entities assumed in the bolshevik and nazi cases.

The Franco dictatorship relied on support from state-organized syndicates and from traditional rightist ruling groups such as the church, the monarchists, and the military. As Linz demonstrated, the single party experiment and other variations invented by Franco after 1936 represented neither a party nor an ideology. The party was created in the "void of political institutionalization."[76] It was a weak party that deliberately eschewed mobilization, and the regime supported this policy. Franco's major political appeal derived, of course, from his role in the Civil War and from the caudillo mystique. But as in any praetorian autocracy, the military became a key force, which obliged Franco to seek its cooperation. He also took the obvious step of creating the political police, the instrument of traditional autocracy.[77]

Franco's Spain lies on the dividing line between classical and modern authoritarianism. The major requirements of modern authoritarianism are the mobilization of masses, a single influential party, and the existence of parallel and auxiliary structures. All of

74. Ibid., pp. 142–45.
75. Linz, "From Falange to Movimiento-Organización," pp. 142–46.
76. Ibid., pp. 162–65.
77. Linz, "An Authoritarian Regime," pp. 267–68.

these only partially existed in Franco's corporate regime. Nevertheless, Franco's regime was modern in the sense that it has the *mentality* of modern authoritarianism: a single party, a corporate state, ideology, and domination by a charismatic leader. The corporate authoritarian state is a controlled mobilization system (not in Linz's version wherein mobilization is not continuous but only occurs early in the regime), but in the sense that the regime deliberately restricts mobilization of the masses. Franco's concept of control is different from those of the party-state and the Nazi political police state because he was not concerned about the future role of the masses. Instead, he guaranteed the survival of his dictatorship by demobilizing and establishing a corporate state—an alliance between nonpopulist, military, Catholic, conservative, professional, and syndicalist groups which he totally dominated.

The nonparty legitimacy claimed by Brazil is similar to that of Franco's Spain and Salazar's Portugal.[78] Both were defensive modernization systems.[79] Franco did not establish his regime in 1936 in order to arrest the modernization process; however, three decades of very modest growth under authoritarian rule made it advisable for Franco to mollify the new modernizing classes by instituting defensive modernization (a term Schmitter correctly applies to authoritarian Brazil).[80]

Corporatism is not the same as limited pluralism. It is a system of organized coalitions of corporatist groups. However, if pluralism is construed to mean that the state or the party elite organize and dominate social and interest groups, then the Bolsheviks, Nazis, and Fascists encouraged limited pluralism. Franco's Spain was socially but not legally pluralistic and elitist. Salazar's Portugal and modern Brazil had and have that kind of limited pluralism. The

78. Ibid., pp. 241–42.
79. Linz, "The Future of an Authoritarian Situation," p. 235.
80. Schmitter, "The 'Portugalization' of Brazil," in *Authoritarian Brazil*, ed. Alfred Stepan (New Haven: Yale University Press, 1973), pp. 206–07. On mentalities see Juan Linz, "Totalitarian and Authoritarian Regimes" in *Handbook of Political Science*, ed. F. Greenstein and N. Polsky (Reading, Mass.: Addison-Wesley, 1975), vol. 3, *Macropolitical Theory*, pp. 204–74. The idea of mentality (a terribly unsatisfactory and vague concept) originates with Theodor Geiger, *Die Sociale Schichtung des deutschen Volkes* (Stuttgart: F. Enke, 1932).

very nature of the corporate state is that dictatorship organizes social and economic interests under the umbrella of a national
syndicate—the corporate council or cabinet. In Franco's Spain and
Salazar's Portugal, the corporate council was pluralistic only in the
sense that it represented class and functional interests.

New Corporatism. Although an extension of the old model, the new
corporatist state is characterized by a low degree of political participation by reactive interest groups. While old corporatism recruited members of the prebureaucratic oligarchy and the extended family into the political system, the new model establishes
a patrimonial type of relationship within and between corporatist
and bureaucratic structures. Authority remains patrimonial-
clientalistic; the organization, however, is modern, bureaucratic,
and even technocratic.

The corporatist state intervenes in the society to a limited extent; it is a model of governance. It "refers to a particular set of
policies and institutional arrangements for structuring interest
representation."[81] In my view, it is both an historical continuity as,
for example, the Franco-Salazar model, and a response to a crisis
situation as, for example, the Latin American model. It is both a
reflection of the existing society and a producer of new types of
authoritarianism. The old corporatism was conservative, royalist,
and an expression of historical authoritarianism. The new corporatism, as analyzed by Schmitter, Linz, Stepan, and Kaufman-
Purcell, represents modern authoritarianism.

Old corporatism differs from the new in two fundamental structural aspects. The new corporatist state responds to the crisis of
modernization by replacing old oligarchies and liberal politicians
who failed to manage the crisis with the military. New corporatism
in Latin America, with the exception of Mexico, is almost incon-
ceivable without the active intervention and continuous support of
the military, at least after the initial years. Stepan suggests why, in
his view, the military has become the strategic elite which responds "to the perception of impending crisis."[82] The military elite
can install the new corporatist model only by adapting a new defi-

    81. Alfred Stepan, *The State and Society: Peru in Comparative Perspec-
tive* (Princeton, N.J.: Princeton University Press, 1978), p. 46.
    82. Ibid., pp. 127–36.

nition of professionalism. "Old professionalism," as described by Huntington, is concerned with external security; it is highly specialized, with a restricted action; and its socialization is neutral, that is, the general attitude is apolitical. New professionalism responds primarily to problems of internal security. Military skills are desirable but oriented toward police and managerial functions, and their scope of action is unrestricted.[83]

John Fitch's study of the Ecuadorian army from 1948 to 1966 also stresses the importance of psychological and institutional changes in the rise of new professionalism. In the Ecuadorian army, the degree of professionalism and developmental ambition changed the military's aspirations and made it interventionist if not reformist.[84]

Characteristics of the New Professional. I have classified this type of authoritarianism as corporate praetorian.[85] Stepan, Schmitter, and O'Donnell distinguish two subtypes of Latin America's new corporatism: inclusionary corporatism, in which the state elite attempts to forge a new equilibrium between state and society through policies that utilize new economic models and involve the working classes; and exclusionary corporatism, in which the state-society equilibrium is regulated by use of coercive policies and the restructuring of salient working class groups. The former incorporates new political and economic forces into the system; the latter excludes any autonomous organizations and groups. Most significantly, the former allies itself with the national bourgeoisie, the latter with the international bourgeoisie and technocracy. Inclusionary corporatism characteristically considers the old oligarchy and foreign capital its enemies; the enemies of the exclusionary type are populists, radical leaders, and the autonomously organized working classes. One type tries to derive its legitimacy from populism, the other from having established order.

These analytic distinctions help classify the two types of new corporatism with greater precision. They do not, however, conflict

83. Ibid., pp. 129–33; see especially table 41.1, p. 130.
84. John Samuel Fitch, *The Military Coup D'Etat as a Political Process: Ecuador 1948–1966* (Baltimore: Johns Hopkins University Press, 1977), pp. 10–12.
85. Perlmutter, *The Military and Politics in Modern Times,* chaps. 1, 4, 6.

with labeling both systems as corporatist-praetorian: the military plays the key role, actually demarcating the lines between the inclusionary and exclusionary corporatist types. At this point, the linkage between new corporatism and praetorianism becomes a key explanatory tool. Thus, Nasserite etatist and oligarchic praetorianism shares the authoritarian orientations of exclusionary corporatism but not the types of relationships predominant in this model.

To group the more complex and economically advanced Latin American regimes separately from less advanced Arab and North African regimes is to relegate praetorianism to the regimes of the Middle East and Africa. Corporatism, inclusionary and exclusionary, consequently becomes identified with the more advanced military regimes of Latin America. Comparatively speaking, both share praetorian and authoritarian orientations, which means that the military's propensity to intervene is real. Thus, if one wishes to distinguish among modern authoritarian regimes, structures, and practices, one could lump together the corporatist and the praetorian models that, compared to the mobilizational authoritarianism of communist and fascist regimes, represent less-developed forms of authoritarianism. According to O'Donnell, who classifies Latin American political systems according to their levels of modernization, there are two types of corporate authoritarianism: bureaucratic and populist. The distinction is useful but insufficient, since it includes praetorianism, the quality that applies to all such regimes at least in Latin America. Corporate-praetorianism is a political system in which the corporatist group is dependent on the state and in which the military is the arbiter of the corporatist conglomerate, with greater autonomy because it can intervene.

Bureaucratic Authoritarianism: A New Concept? The general thesis of the innovators of the concept (its meaning varies from author to author)[86] is that bureaucratic authoritarianism differs considerably from corporatism and fascism.[87] It is "thought of as a

86. Authored by G. O'Donnell, *Modernization and Bureaucratic Authoritarianism* (Berkeley: Institute of International Studies, 1975). For different versions see David Collier, ed., *The New Authoritarianism in Latin America* (Princeton, N.J.: Princeton University Press, 1979).

87. Collier, ed., *The New Authoritarianism*, pp. 33–60, 285–318.

type of authoritarianism characterized by a self-avowedly technocratic, bureaucratic, nonpersonalistic approach to policy making
and problem solving."[88] These authors, who are knowledgeable
about Latin America and distinguished social scientists, in my
view invoke the corporatist authoritarian type. Cardoso argues
that bureaucratic authoritarianism is differentiated from Italian or
German fascism (not distinguishing nazism from fascism) because
the bureaucratic authoritarian system aspires to produce and produces apathy, fears mobilization, dispenses for the most part with
political parties, and fears reactions from lower strata and favors
the middle strata. All of these characteristics, however, are clearly
praetorian. In fact, Cardoso admits that "The army, as . . . [a]
guarantor of the authoritarian order, . . . prefers a 'technical' sup-
portive relationship between the state and social groups, rather
than a relationship based on alliances with broad social groups."[89]
This is one of the finest definitions of corporatist authoritarianism.
Collier reiterates that "Argentina and Brazil were ruled by the military as an institution, rather than exclusively by individual military rulers . . . [and the] military adopt a technocratic bureaucratic
approach to policy making."[90]

This reiterates our theses that what is modern about modern
authoritarianism is the technique of governing, ruling, and administering. Bureaucratic authoritarianism is an unfulfilled and
confusing concept since modern corporatism and the modern military in nonauthoritarian regimes are also technocratic, nonper-
sonal organizations related to the *Gesellschaft* ("society") rather
than the *Gemeinschaft* ("community") concept of politics. The difference is that under bureaucratic authoritarianism, the military
rules. The theory of bureaucratic authoritarianism is tantamount
to arguing that no politics exist in bureaucratic authoritarian systems for mechanistic, nonorganic, pseudopolitical relationships
between state and society.[91] This is not true of *any* political system,

88. Ibid., p. 400.
89. Cardoso, "On the Characterization of Authoritarian Regimes in
Latin America," in *The New Authoritarianism*, ed. David Collier (Princeton,
N.J.: Princeton University Press, 1979), p. 36.
90. David Collier, "Introduction," in *The New Authoritarianism*, ed.
David Collier (Princeton, N.J.: Princeton University Press, 1979), p. 4.
91. According to Collier's and Cardoso's analysis, in the bureaucratic

authoritarian or otherwise. Corporate praetorianism is precisely what Collier and Cardoso describe: the military institution—a corporatist, modern, large-scale organization of the modern nation state—is a guarantor (praetorian) of society and politics. The apolitical argument is fallacious. In communist, fascist, and nazi authoritarianism, the party or the party-state is the chief instrument of political power; in corporatist praetorian regimes, the military institution is the central political instrument (ruler, or arbiter). That is the difference between communism, fascism, and bureaucratic authoritarianism. What is missing in the bureaucratic authoritarian systems, and in all praetorian and corporatist regimes, is not politics but the political prerequisite for the seizure and establishment of parallel and auxiliary political structures, the vehicles of authoritarianism. Under no condition can the military establish political parallel and auxiliary structures, before, during, or after the seizure of power as long as the initiative for the seizure of power and its maintenance remains with the military organization (run by individuals in praetorian tyrannies and oligarchies and by the military institution in corporate praetorianism). Several military regimes have tried to form parallel and auxiliary structures after the seizure of power; all, with the exception of Kemalist Turkey, failed. The authoritarian politics of the communist, nazi and fascist systems are clearly centered in and around the institutionalized instruments of the seizure of power: the party, the army, and the state. What differentiates praetorian and, to some extent, corporatist regimes from other modern authoritarian systems is that their foci of power are neither clear nor institutionalized. Sometimes they are monopolized by military men, other times by the military institution or by alliances of the military-technocracy or the upper-class bourgeoisie. The last instance almost describes classical praetorianism. In Rome, the senate, the leading families, the equestrian and the banking classes ruled for a long period during the Republic and the Empire.[92] The

---

authoritarian system, the military may either have veto power or wield power directly.

92. See Ronald Syme, *The Roman Revolution*, (Oxford: Oxford University Press, 1939), pp. 11–28.

guarantor of the system was the oligarchy and the military, hence the concept of praetorianism.

The politics of corporate praetorianism is neither organic nor classical, that is, the society and state are not based on broad alliance of social groups as in pluralistic democracy. This is true of all modern authoritarian regimes. Some, like communist and nazi regimes, are more efficient in eliciting public response; others, like the Fascists, are less so; and some, the praetorian type, for example, are not at all. The type of political intervention produced by corporate praetorian regimes is distinct from the all-inclusive interventionist party of the party-state. Corporate praetorianism is indifferent to social action, or at least places restrictions on it, while communism and fascism are dedicated to mobilization and to destroying the old social and political classes. Yet the Soviet, Nazi, and Fascist efforts to create new men and new societies were as unsuccessful as those of the bureaucratic authoritarian regime. The difference is that the former tried and failed to change the nature of men and the nature of politics while bureaucratic authoritarianism is unconcerned with such noble endeavors. Unlike Portuguese corporatism, Latin American systems are hierarchical, mechanical, technical, and inorganic. Organic bonds to the state, which are at the roots of the old corporatism and of communism, are not manifest in any praetorian system including the bureaucratic authoritarian, or corporate praetorian, type. The institutions of bureaucratic authoritarianism are the executive and the techno-bureaucracy. Surely the relationship between the techno-bureaucracy and the military is political, and even Collier concludes that in the end, "The military has veto power over 'big decisions'—the most important being control of political succession."[93] This corresponds to the function of the politburo in communist systems. Making big decisions is a political, not an administrative, act. In corporate praetorianism (bureaucratic authoritarianism) "they [the military] are not necessarily involved in decision making regarding the economy or other important issues."[94] The military delegates this authority to the executive but

93. Collier, *The New Authoritarianism*, p. 31.
94. Ibid., p. 32.

this is also a political act. What distinguishes political authority from other types of social and economic authority and organizations is clearly the crux of the issue. The established institutions and procedures of politics in the authoritarian regime differ from those of pluralist-liberal-democratic systems whether capitalist or socialist. The *types* of political structures established to conduct, negotiate, and implement politics and policies distinguish authoritarian regimes. The bureaucratic authoritarian model is unrealistic in the sense that it implies the existence of a system which has no way to interact with social groups. If there is no organic or other bond between the state and society, supposedly there are no politics or negotiations between state and society. Thus, in bureaucratic authoritarian systems, the arrangement of power and authority are authoritarian and bureaucratic, but this only explains the nature of the arrangement, not its substance. The substance of politics in authoritarian regimes is conducted by their institutionalized parallel and auxiliary structures; in this sense the military institution in the corporate praetorian Latin American regime is a surrogate auxiliary structure, with the difference that it is the only arbitrating political force. In the corporate authoritarian regime, political space is limited to the techno-military institution. Truly, the political structures—the military and the executive—in the bureaucratic authoritarian or corporate praetorian regime are not "the locus wherein the tensional forces of society are related."[95] In this sense, it is just another type of authoritarianism, or another type of authoritarian politics.

The Praetorian Model

In a modern praetorian state the military tends to intervene and has the potential to dominate the executive. The political conditions in such states favor the development of the military as the core group and encourage its expectations of becoming a ruling class and a political elite.

In several developing states, the military functions as it did in the patrimonial states; it provides an arena for political conflict

95. Sheldon Wolin, *Politics and Vision* (Boston: Little Brown, 1960), p. 7.

and ambition, and it threatens the legitimate authority. But modern praetorianism differs significantly from the patrimonial model. First, whereas the patrimonial military represented and defended the existing regime's legitimacy, the modern military challenges that legitimacy and offers to substitute its authority. Second, in historical praetorianism the relationship of authority between the military establishment and the political order is based on tradition, but in modern praetorianism that relationship is based on a legal-rational orientation.

In a praetorian state political authority is not institutionalized and the social or ethnic-religious system is fragmented. There is a wide gap between political order and mobilization. Compared to other political, bureaucratic, social, and economic structures, the military establishment displays the greatest degree of institutionalization. As a result, it has the potential to dominate the state. Nevertheless, lack of an institutionalized authority and a fragmented society do not cause military praetorianism to evolve. Praetorianism occurs when the military elite, or a segment of it, seeks to maximize its political influence in the absence of a serious political and structural rival and an effective elite organization. *The orientation of the modern military in the praetorian state is to maximize its influence and involvement in politics.*

Military influence in praetorian politics takes at least three forms: military coups, military regimes, and the drive for influence in national security policy making. By military coups, I mean those defined as "occurring whenever members of the regular armed forces remove or attempt to remove a state's chief executive through the use or threat of the use of force."[96] By military regimes, I mean regimes dominated by a coalitional military oligarchy. Modern military oligarchies are not purely military in composition; they are coalitions, that is, civil-military regimes. However, the modern military regime is different from the historical version in that the former seeks mass political support. Such regimes can be personalist, oligarchic, or corporatist. In most cases, the only political support the military solicits or obtains is from civilian

96. Amos Perlmutter, "The Praetorian State and the Praetorian Army," *Comparative Politics* 1 (April 1969): 384.

bureaucracies, social-political elites or corporatist groups: it is not popular or electoral support. Military regimes that do seek electoral support at best achieve only plebiscitary support. In any case, no military regime can rely solely on legitimate electoral and popular approval; it must use coercion, and, most significantly, most civil-military regimes must depend on the support of the whole military establishment to survive.

Types of Modern Military Praetorianism. Modern military praetorianism has three subtypes: autocratic, oligarchic, and corporatist. Military autocracy is simple military tyranny: the unchecked personal authority of a military officer. Military oligarchy is a political system in which executive power is wielded by a few individuals, mostly military men. The chief executive is either a former military man who is now a civilian or a civilian figurehead whose support comes exclusively from the military. The only intrinsic difference between the military oligarchy and the military tyranny is the number of rulers involved.

Corporate praetorianism is characterized by combined military-civilian rule. Governmental authority resides in a coalition of military men and civilians—bureaucrats, managers, and technocrats—who govern with little or no external political control. There may be a civilian majority, and the supreme head may even be a civilian who does not possess military skills.

The distinction between oligarchical and corporate praetorianism is derived from different socioeconomic and political-institutional conditions. On the whole, the corporate type is a regime that rules over a relatively developed society where socioeconomic groups are corporatively organized and are linked to the corporatist state. The oligarchical type represents a poorly stratified society and the absence, or near absence, of organized and autonomous economic interest groups and of structures for political articulation and interest aggregation.

The corporate praetorian regime makes it costly for society to resist the interests of corporatist groups that are supported by the state and especially by the military. Political bargaining is conducted between organized groups; the military either arbitrates or dictates policies. In the oligarchical type, the military is more pow-

erful than other organized groups, and it allies itself with a
bureaucracy which becomes either a silent or a junior partner.
Power is dependent solely on the military.

Corporate praetorian regimes link the society with the state.
They are products of industrialization and modernization and exist
in a number of Latin American states.[97] Corporate praetorianism is
a political system in which organizations officially represent private interests and the range of state activities is wide. The state
performs managerial, bureaucratic, and technocratic functions
and is both repressive and efficient.

A corporate military regime has restricted political support and
political mobilization. The major source of support must come
from the military establishment. In the case of a military tyranny,
electoral exercises are not even contemplated. A military oligarchy, in contrast, makes a considerable effort to create a facade of
electoral support but calls elections infrequently.

The corporate military regime seeks additional political support outside of the military among the different state-linked corporate groups. It is sincere in calling elections, even if the choice is
limited to an executive chosen by the military. This type of regime
might tolerate national political institutions and structures, such
as parliaments, parties, and pressure groups, that are not oriented
toward military rule and control. It also tolerates local governments and other authorities that are not directly dominated or
directed by the military.

One example of corporate praetorianism is the Brazilian mili-

97. On Corporatism, bureaucratic authoritarianism, praetorian-
corporatism, and populist-corporatism in Latin America, see O'Donnell,
Modernization and Bureaucratic Authoritarianism; James Malloy, ed., *Au-
thoritarianism and Corporatism in Latin America* (Pittsburgh: University of
Pittsburgh Press, 1977); see also Alfred Stepan, ed., *Authoritarian Brazil;*
Peter Cleaves, *Bureaucratic Politics and Administration in Chile* (Berkeley:
University of California Press, 1974); Fitch, *The Military Coup D'Etat;* Susan
Kaufman Purcell, *The Mexican Profit Sharing Decision* (Berkeley: Univer-
sity of California Press, 1975); Kenneth Erickson, *The Brazilian Corporate
State and Working Class Politics* (Berkeley: University of California Press,
1977); and Karen Remner, "The Dynamics of Authoritarian Regimes: The
Case of Brazil," (Paper delivered at LASA/ASA Conference, Houston, Texas,
November 1977).

POLITICAL DYNAMICS
tary regime of the early 1970s. "Power basically remained with the
armed forces, except for economic policy making, which is shared
between the military, selected technocrats, and to a lesser extent,
businessmen. Institutions outside the armed forces have been
created and disregarded constantly, leaving the military with the
ultimate power."[98]

Since the line between oligarchic and corporate praetorianism
is permeable, this dichotomy is made for heuristic purposes. The
confusion over which type of regime one is looking at comes from
rhetoric and from the various interpretations and explanations of
praetorian regimes; when the frame of reference is narrowed, the
distinctions will emerge. To circumvent the analytical and theoretical model, one would have to assign time sequences and place the
regime in time and space. Yet clearly, alternation between oligarchic and corporatist regimes is not uncommon in Latin America. In
fact, corporatist regimes incorporate elements of oligarchism more
often than vice versa. The dynamics of governing make the two
praetorian subtypes more permeable than the analytical distinction indicates. Nevertheless, the distinction between oligarchic and
corporatist praetorianism results from different types of elite and
social conflict formations and different levels of economic and
political development. These elements distinguish Argentinian and
Brazilian from Egyptian and Iraqi praetorianism.

Political Support, Mobilization, and Auxiliary Structures. The most
important source of political support for the praetorian regime is
the military establishment. In corporate praetorianism, additional
support can come from such corporatist groups as the bureaucracy,
the church, labor unions, and the technocracy. The military arbitrates (and thus rules) between the corporatist organizations that
compete to exploit the state. Clearly, without the support of the
military establishment or one of its major factions, no praetorian
regime can survive.

As mentioned earlier, the type of political support is what
differentiates corporate and oligarchic from tyrannical praeto-

98. Alfred Stepan, "The Future," in *Authoritarian Brazil*, ed. Alfred
Stepan (New Haven: Yale University Press, 1973), p. 235.

rianism. The latter only wants the support of the military, while the former want to widen their bases of support. However, in the area of economic modernization, the corporate and oligarchic types are actively committed to industrialization and economic advancement, although they pursue these goals while restricting the growth of alternative political groups. The praetorian systems in Brazil, Argentina, Chile, and Peru are committed to agrarian and industrial modernization and even to social and tax reforms. To some extent, this is true of Egypt since Nasser. Other praetorian regimes, such as the personalist type, are less committed to economic modernization.

The three most interesting structural political innovations of modern authoritarian praetorianism are the army-party (a party created by harnessing a popular or radical party to the military regime), the military executive, and the corporatist-military cabinet conglomerate. The first two are auxiliary structures designed to widen the base of political support, help sustain the praetorian regime, and create structures and procedures that legitimate the regime. They are not instruments of mobilization.

The army-party and the military executive are found under oligarchic praetorianism, which is most prevalent in the Arab Middle East.[99] Here, the mechanism for executive control is the revolutionary command council, which is the instrument of conquest and power; in other words, it is the executive committee of the coup. Once in power, it assumes different forms, variously calling itself the presidential office, the cabinet, or the council. In all cases, however, its motivation is the same—the continuation of political monopoly. Although the new regime may create a political party or conquer an established one, this party will be kept

99. For the literature on military praetorianism in the Middle East, see Eliezer Be'eri, *Army Officers in Arab Politics and Society* (New York: Praeger, 1970); P. J. Vatikiotis, *The Egyptian Army in Politics* (Bloomington: University of Indiana Press, 1966); R. Hrair Dekmedjian, *Egypt Under Nasir* (Albany: State University of New York Press, 1971); and Perlmutter, *Egypt: The Praetorian State* (New Brunswick, N.J.: Transaction, 1974). See also Raymond W. Baker, *Egypt's Uncertain Revolution under Sadat and Nasser* (Cambridge, Mass.: Harvard University Press, 1978) and P. J. Vatikiotis, *Nasser and His Generation* (London: Croom Helm, 1978).

weak so that the revolutionary command council can dominate the regime. The function of the weak single party has never been to mobilize the masses, as demonstrated by the histories of Ayub's Basic Democracy, Nasser's semibureaucratic cadre, and the Arab Socialist Union. The function of such groups is to assist the praetorian oligarchy in running the state, whether by dominating the state's elephantine bureacracy as in Egypt or by subduing traditional opponents and splinter groups as in Syria.[100] The Liberation Rally, Nasser's major effort at creating a single party, was to serve at first as the junta's chief propaganda vehicle. Primarily occupied with pamphleteering and proselytizing for the Nasserite Egyptian revolution in the countryside and in mosques, it ended in failure in 1954. Arab military regimes have been more successful propagandists, however, than other praetorian regimes. Those in Africa, for example, have been notably deficient in this department.

With the exception of these innovations—the revolutionary command council and the weak single party—no other parallel and auxiliary structures have been introduced by modern praetorians. In fact, the general inability to institutionalize other political structures is closely linked to the failure of the oligarchic and corporatist praetorian to institutionalize the military executive and the military party. Thus, even the military oligarchies depend on one man's charisma—Nasser's, for instance—or on the political skills of a Sadat, Assad, or Ghaddafi. The military tyranny of Amin's, Mobutu's and Bokassa's sub-Saharan African styles made no contribution to parallel or auxiliary structures of modern praetorianism, although they introduced considerable refinements in the practices of torture and terror.

Other innovations of modern authoritarian praetorianism are the bureaucratic authoritarian regime, like those of Brazil from 1964 to 1976, Argentina from 1966 to 1970, and Chile since 1973, and the populist authoritarian regime found in Bolivia, Ecuador, Peru, and in Chile during the Allende period. Both types are characterized by having relatively regular and autonomous governmental structures.[101]

100. Perlmutter, *Military and Politics in Modern Times.*
101. James Malloy, "Authoritarianism and Corporatism in Latin

Modern authoritarian regimes in corporatist Latin America are nonelected governments or governments that have been formally elected but do not have any legal or effective opposition. In each of them, the military establishment is an important consumer of state resources. Such regimes simply represent a specific type of nonelected government-military rule.[102]

America," in *Authoritarianism and Corporatism in Latin America*, ed. James Malloy (Pittsburgh: University of Pittsburgh Press, 1977), p. 305.

102. Summarized from David S. Palmer, "The Politics of Authoritarianism in Spanish America," in *Authoritarianism*, ed. James Malloy, p. 378.

CHAPTER THREE

Authoritarianism and Development

The Political Dynamics of Modern Authoritarianism

So far, comparative definitions and typologies have demonstrated that we cannot usefully generalize about modern authoritarianism and autocracy unless we distinguish between types and analyze each cluster independently. To explain the political dynamics of authoritarian regimes we again divide them into two major groups: stable regimes (the bolshevik, nazi, and fascist types) and unstable regimes (the corporatist and praetorian types). Samuel Huntington argues that the one-party system is the chief characteristic of modern authoritarianism, and he distinguishes between strong (bolshevik, nazi, fascist) and weak (praetorian) one-party systems. He also differentiates authoritarian parties on the basis of relative capacity to expand political power. The strong-weak continuum involves three variables: the legitimation of the system, recruitment of political leadership, and interest aggregation and policy making.[1] I shall take advantage of this classification to explain the dynamics of authoritarianism. However, I consider changes in the structure and dynamics of political authority and mobilization and of the parallel, auxiliary, and propaganda structures to be consequences of the interplay between economic and social forces, political constraints, and, necessarily, of the party's capacity to expand power.

1. S. P. Huntington, "Social and Institutional Dynamics of One-Party Systems," in *Authoritarian Politics in Modern Society*, ed. S. P. Huntington and C. H. Moore (New York: Basic Books, 1970), pp. 3–4.

Highly Institutionalized Authoritarian Systems

Political Dynamics. In authoritarian regimes the momentum of mobilization must be arrested at some point in order for power to be consolidated. To legitimate the ruling elite, the regime must then stabilize, institutionalize, and limit established auxiliary political institutions, which are initially manned by loyalists. However, the recruitment, skills, and orientations of these new political groups are as dependent on the economic and social development of the society as on the polity. Political bureaucratic dynamics encompass the party, the state, and the parallel and auxiliary structures. New types of actors—technocrats, managers, highly skilled bureaucrats, and military professionals—supersede the historical apparatchik-ideologues and join the ruling and strategic elites.

In the communist case, the modern elites are distributed more or less evenly between the party and the state they dominate; they also control the auxiliary structures. In the case of the Nazis, the state came under the influence of the Beamten who commanded an exalted importance unknown since 1918. The Beamten held a wide range of modern skills, while the party was less advanced. In the diplomatic and military services, the better educated and trained professionals served the state while the amateurs served Ribbentrop and his Nazis after 1936. Only a few qualified military professionals served the SS (except for the Waffen SS, a special military unit). In Mussolini's Italy, the modern professionals were employed principally by the state and its corporate structures, while the party was the domain of the old squadrismo-romantic revolutionaries, an elite of predominantly provincial bosses and bullies.

Economic Dynamics. Communist authoritarianism is an archetypal political system dedicated to economic and technocratic modernization. This is true even if authoritarianism has not been efficiently modernized in the Soviet Union.

Although they began as a regressive revolutionary elite, the Nazis redirected their orientation and sought industrialization and modernization as a means of achieving political lebensraum for Germany and of furthering rearmament. Among other things, this pacified the military in the Nazi state and partially reconciled the führer to the state by bringing about a rapprochement with the German middle class and the German generals, diplomats, and industrialists who initially opposed nazism. Thus the dynamics of modernization prompted by Hitler's globalist and racist aspirations created an unholy alliance between the Nazi party and the Nazi state under the führer. Socially, if not ideologically, the old classes and their representatives, whom the early Nazis had wanted to eliminate, came to serve the Nazi state. However, they were not integrated into the party or state; they were exploited for instrumental and pragmatic purposes.[2]

Consolidation of the Nazi regime followed, with the establishment of the one-party system and the institutionalization of Gleichschaltung in economics, defense, and foreign policy. This policy brought two antagonistic organizations, the Nazi party and the Beamten, face to face.[3]

Führerprinzip ("principle of leadership"), which had made Hitler the supreme ruler, inspired the Nazis to hope to take over the state and oust the traditional Beamten, but this did not happen. Because Hitler was fully aware that both the party and the SS would get out of hand, "he increasingly began to emphasize the importance of the State in relation to the Party organization."[4] Hitler tried to gain control of the state both by nazifying the bureaucrats and by placing Nazis within the bureaucracy. "Having got control of the State, the Nazis in State positions then applied themselves to asserting them with total centralization as the ultimate goal. The short-term result was rather to the contrary, a wild growth of new institutions, jurisdictional disputes, and personal conflicts, arising not only out of the conflict between State and Party, but between Nazi and Nazi."[5] Bracher adds:

2. David Schoenbaum, *Hitler's Social Revolution* (New York: Anchor Books, 1966).

3. Karl Bracher, *The German Dictatorship* (New York: Praeger, 1970), p. 228–36.

4. J. Noakes and G. Pridham, *Documents on Nazism: 1919–1945* (New York: Viking Press, 1974), pp. 225–39. Quotation is on p. 233.

5. Schoenbaum, *Hitler's Social Revolution*, p. 197.

The fact that even in the future [after 1933] the party never achieved clear-cut primacy testifies to the ambiguous character of the National Socialist system. The formula of the party issuing orders to the state was true of the Communist one-party state which had smashed the old governmental machinery and the traditional elite structure, although even there the future might see a return to dual structure. But in the Third Reich where traditional and revolutionary elements continued to exist partly fused and partly rivals, the primacy of the party was established only in specific instances; at times it almost seemed as if the opposite were the case, and often enough it was not even the party and the state but rival party bigwigs who found themselves on opposite sides.[6]

Thus, in both the Nazi and Soviet cases, the drive for modernization created the conditions, however different, for the political weakening of the mobilizational party. After 1933, the Nazi party was in decline since it had to share power with the state. During the war, the only effective instruments of power were Hitler's charisma, Goebbels' propaganda machinery and Himmler's system of terror. These forces weakened support for the Nazi party and its secondary elite and enhanced Hitler's dictatorship, since it was he who manipulated the state-party conflicts.

In the USSR, the party led and directed the modern industrial revolution; as a result it became the most powerful source of political power. Nevertheless, the party paid a price. First, the economic instruments of the state and the soviets were strengthened. Second, the power of the political police was weakened. Third, the predominance of the ideologue-apparatchik and the professional revolutionary gave way to the ascendance of modern managerial technocrats and bureaucrats. However, the party did not loosen its control of ideas because that would have threatened its political monopoly, a development that could not be tolerated. The harsh repression of the Czech experiment by the USSR, for example, stemmed at least in part from disapproval of the changing Czech economic philosophy as revealed in a number of reforms.

6. Bracher, *The German Dictatorship*, p. 235.

Richard Lowenthal argues that communism, or my bolshevik model, is a special type of politically forced development, that is, it is a dictatorship of development.[7] Successful modernization is counterposed against the achievement of communist utopia. To catch up with Western nations, economically and militarily, the USSR needs to reeducate the masses. The struggle between utopia and development creates a conflict over policy between party and state professionals, ideologues and technocrats, apparatchiks and managers. Hence, the parallel party-state institutions are maintained at a cost to both. Elite dualism over policy, ideology, party modernity, and change are the demiurges of political cleavage in the bolshevik model and the source of inner party conflict.[8]

The decline of the party's revolutionary function and the modernizers' rising prominence heightens party conflict and raises questions as to the party's future role and stability. However strong it still is, the party's relative decline in legitimacy is the consequence of political and economic dynamics of some seventy years of Bolshevik authoritarianism.

Social Dynamics. Group conflict is as evident in the USSR as anywhere else. Nevertheless, political groups and interest politics in the bolshevik model are formal structures and not autonomous constructions because there is no free interchange and expression of ideas and group interests. H. Gordon Skilling characterized political groups in the bolshevik model as part of a pyramid of combined state and party power. At the top are leadership groups, below them official and bureaucratic groups (the strategic elite), and still lower is the intellectual-scientific group. The lowest group of all are the workers and farmers.[9]

Such cleavages exist, but the group theorists analyzing the USSR unfortunately confuse an analysis of elite layers, or of the

7. Richard Lowenthal, "Development vs. Utopia in Communist Policy," in *Change in Communist Systems*, ed. Chalmers Johnson (Stanford: Stanford University Press, 1970), pp. 33–116.

8. Ibid., pp. 54–57.

9. H. Gordon Skilling, "Group Conflict and Political Change," in *Change in Communist Systems*, ed. Chalmers Johnson (Stanford: Stanford University Press, 1970), pp. 215–17.

party's circulation of elites, with a group theory. Elites are neither groups nor structures. In the communist model, they are linked to the oligopolistic political structure, but never to a market or extrapolitical formation, which association is the essence of group theory. Bureaucrats and bureaucracies are not groups because there is nothing societal, in the classical sense, about bureaucracies. Sheldon Wolin settled this issue by demonstrating the intellectual fallacy of sublimating society to organization. Let us not confuse the analysis of the authoritarian states' grand organization and their raisons d'être with communal or even societal orientations. The party, army, police, and economic structures within the oligopolistic USSR are not groups, and they are not pluralistic. They are oligopolistic elites struggling for power within hegemonic political structures. C. Wright Mills's power elite theory, which states that there are linkages between elites' institutional and corporate structures, fits the bolshevik model perfectly even though it only emphasizes its organization and not its communal nature. Group conflict is not confined to the institutions of the party-state; elite conflict is. "According to group-conflict theorists," writes Bailes, "a society such as the Soviet Union is far from harmonious; nor is all power monopolized by a single unified group. Behind the facade of formal unity and a single party, intense conflict often rages over disparate values, interests, and policies."[10] But these are conflicts among elites, not groups. Thus, dichotomous totalitarian and group-conflict models have been employed to explain the social, and of course the political, dynamics of the party-state in the USSR. Although no general consensus has been reached, the two models have been refined and improved considerably.[11] Another model, closer to the totalitarian version, is that of the bureaucratic school.[12] "The USSR is best understood as a large, complex

10. Kendall E. Bailes, *Technology and Society under Lenin and Stalin* (Princeton, N.J.: Princeton University Press, 1978), p. 12.

11. Jerry Hough, *The Soviet Union and Social Science Theory* (Cambridge, Mass.: Harvard University Press, 1977).

12. Alfred Meyer, *The Soviet Political System: An Interpretation* (New York: Random House, 1965), pp. 477–78. See also T. H. Rigby and Allen Kass, "The Administered Society: Totalitarianism without Terror," *World Politics* 16 (July 1964): 558–75.

bureaucracy comparable in its structure and functioning to giant corporations, armies, government agencies, and similar institutions in the West. It shares with such bureaucracies many principles of organization and patterns of management."[13]

In an effort to reconcile both schools, Bailes has introduced a new model that synthesizes the totalitarian and group-conflict models. "A new model gradually took shape, which attempts not only to synthesize elements from totalitarian and group-conflict models, but to add elements previously neglected. In the area of social cohesion, such elements include an emphasis not only on the coercive—or totalitarian—means of enforcing social cohesion, but also on the degree to which shared values and interests led at times to voluntary cohesion and initiative among some of the groups analyzed."[14] The role of inter- and intra-class conflicts—the dynamics between modern technology and bureaucracy—is emphasized. Thus the totalitarian party also represents a social structure that contains forces for cohesive action and forces for social conflict which can lead to dissolution or transformation.[15]

The extent of the party apparatus in the contemporary USSR is awesome. Close to 400,000 apparatchiks run the party and, ultimately, the state. Most significantly, the party deems education so crucial that it makes concerted and successful efforts to recruit the better-educated classes. The influence of the technocratic intelligentsia on the party and the state is clear: the higher the party-state organ, the better educated the staff members. Obviously, the so-called mass participation system actually favors the better-educated classes. Sociopolitical activities are not as popular as are techno-bureaucratic ones.[16] The importance of the party organizational department, which was created to manipulate the cadres and control social positions, demonstrates that the party-state has

13. Meyer, *The Soviet Political System.*
14. Bailes, *Technology and Society,* p. 13.
15. Ibid., p. 8.
16. Much of the preceding discussion relies on valuable information found in Mervyn Mathews, *Class and Society in Soviet Russia* (New York: Walker, 1972), pp. 213–54. On party membership, see T. H. Rigby, Communist Party Membership (Princeton, N.J.: Princeton University Press, 1968).

exchanged its Marxist egalitarianism for a technocratic ethos. Political mobility is now achieved by securing a high technocratic position in the party-state. The only challengers to this elite are the Russian intellectuals, who are the only relatively autonomous social group in the bolshevik system but who have little power. Nevertheless, the modernization of the bolshevik system and the emergence of conflict among the institutional elite, even though confined to the party-state, has clearly weakened such auxiliary structures as the political police and the agitprop systems.

Although the institutionalization of parallel bodies has created a wider arena for political cleavage and elite conflicts, the party monopolizes policy decision making and access to information. The dilemma for bolshevik authoritarianism still is that, as Lowenthal put it, although "the conscious purpose of a totalitarian dictatorship is to change social structure without changing the political system, the planned social change results inevitably in unintended and indeed unforeseen political change."[17] The major feature of bolshevik institutionalization, however modified and "pluralized," is "an institutional monopoly of policy decision, organization and information of the ruling party and the freeing of the state from all legal limitations in the exercise of its tasks."[18] Not only has the dictatorship of the Communist party not resisted change, but it has set itself up as the command post for modernization and change.

The Nazi case clearly illustrates the weaknesses and strengths involved in changing society. The Nazi party, before seizing power, was dedicated to destroying the educated middle classes, the pillar of the German bourgeoisie. It succeeded partly through physical annihilation, partly through forced emigration, and partly through disenfranchisement. Romantic Nazi rebels, Freikorps, SA revolutionaries, and leftist National Socialists (the Strasser brothers, for example), were eliminated or rendered politically marginal. The only political powers that remained after the takeover were Hitler, his propaganda, and the SS machine. Hitler's rhetoric, his Alte Kämpfer followers, and other party apparatus were an-

17. Lowenthal, "Development vs. Utopia," p. 109.
18. Ibid., p. 108.

tibourgeois in their ethos but not in their actions. If bourgeois style refers to the way one acquires property and spends money, then Hitler and company were petit bourgeois Germans. Only their rhetoric was couched in antibourgeois, lower middle class language.

The Third Reich was a house divided against itself: a feeling of conflict permeated the party. National Socialism, the system designed to make the world safe for small businessmen, farmers, and townspeople, could not be achieved in an industrial state. As a result, the Nazis had to pursue a policy of rapprochement with their class enemies—the industrialists, generals, and diplomats whom the Nazi movement was expected to destroy. "What held things together," writes Schoenbaum, "was a combination of ideology and social dynamics on a foundation of charisma and terror."[19] Nazi Germany was an industrial and bourgeois society in a state of arrested development. Unlike the situation in the USSR, neither party nor state could change this predicament: the Nazis had to rely on their traditional enemies. "In a revolution arising from their increasing awareness of the situation, the pillars of society— the Junkers, the industrialists, the Bildungsburgertum—joined forces with their own enemies to pull down the roof that hitherto sheltered them."[20]

Between 1933 and 1940, the Nazi regime oversaw a bourgeois-capitalist industrial system devoted to preparation for war. The Nazi party did not play the same role as the Bolshevik party. In fact, the political dynamics of this era, with the exception of the ouster of the Jews and the beginnings of political repression and concentration camps, were not totalitarian. Group and economic activities were relatively free and open although under the party's shadow. Shopkeepers, peasants, and workers benefited from the war because they profited from industrial-military production. The fact that no arena was open to them for autonomous political expression and activity represented the essence of the Nazi dictatorship.

The Nazi model was the only authoritarian regime in a highly

19. Schoenbaum, *Hitler's Social Revolution*, pp. 275–79.
20. Ibid., p. 288.

developed industrial society in which the economic system was not entirely state-owned. It was not dominated by the party because the state directed the economy. The Beamten classes were relatively autonomous under Hitler's rule. But unlike the Soviet Union, the führer, not the party, held a political monopoly. The terror machinery of the USSR through Stalinist times was directed more against the party than against the larger society; in Nazi Germany during the war, it was directed more against external enemies than against the domestic population. In Germany, the society was fragmented, political censorship was widespread, and the party, if it had ever been united, was permanently divided after 1933. But it never split, as it might have in the Soviet Union, nor did it become a new party of technocrats; party members were unable to compete with the highly educated and efficient technocratic civil servants. The old fighters and schemers were not replaced although they became marginal during the regime's later years. The industrialists, generals, diplomats, and Beamten tried to control the machinery of the state at the price of a bitter and unending conflict with Hitler, which they never won. It was not the party that defeated them, but Hitler himself with the party's support. In the meantime, the Beamten and Nazi Gauleiters competed for power; the SS continually tried to infiltrate and terrorize the military.[21] Even Hitler did not succeed in taming the corporate Prussian military machine, although he might have done so if his regime had not come to a catastrophic end so quickly. The military, though subservient, did attempt a few unsuccessful coups. No state, party, or social group ever achieved domination or hegemony in Hitler's Germany. The dual system functioned without a decisive victory for one group or another, even if instrumentally the state did triumph.

I left the analysis of the dynamics of fascist authoritarianism to the end of this section. I have great difficulties in labeling the fascist regime as highly institutionalized. It is debatable whether Mussolini's fascism would be placed fairly in a category between institutionalized and noninstitutionalized. But fascism's in-

21. Edward Peterson, *The Limits of Hitler's Power* (Princeton, N.J.: Princeton University Press, 1968), p. 435.

stitutionalization can be discerned by examining fascist economic doctrines, programs, and achievements. Gregor demonstrates the Fascists' successful embarcation on a policy of economic and social mobilization. Fascist development revealed a high degree of institutionalization and organizational flexibility, adaptability, and complexity. The most convincing proof of its economic institutionalization is its policy toward labor, which evolved "out of the interaction between Fascist commitments and the contingencies that characterized the social, economic, and political circumstances of the years between 1919 and 1925."[22] The syndicalist and Marxist origins of fascism fathered the Fascists' economic and social attitude toward labor. In the 1920s, for example, Mussolini and the Fascists supported workers' occupations of factories, even if only under certain restricted conditions.[23]

By expanding fascist syndicalism in 1920, Mussolini benefited for the first time from working class support. The fascists organized both agricultural and industrial workers, and by 1922 the *Corporazioni Nazionali,* an organization with some half million membership under fascist auspices, became a serious challenger to the traditional Farm Labor association, the *Federterra,* with half as many members.[24] The new fascist syndicates were a considerable success, enhancing Mussolini's power and advancing fascist mobilization by appealing to proletarian aspirations. Fascist syndicates were not organized solely as working class, wage-oriented, self defense associations; they were also instruments of national consciousness, dedicated to "national production" rather than class struggle. Not unlike the Bolsheviks, the Fascists finally harnessed the working class associations to the state.

When we turn to Fascist social policy, again we find that contrary to the classical liberal interpretation of fascism, Mussolini was actively engaged in social legislation.[25] Living conditions,

22. For a comprehensive and detailed analysis of fascist labor policy see A. James Gregor, *Italian Fascism and Developmental Dictatorship* (Princeton, N.J.: Princeton University Press, 1979), pp. 172–213.

23. Ibid., p. 173.

24. Ibid., pp. 183–89.

25. On the comparative analysis of fascist and bolshevik models, see Gregor, *Italian Fascism and Developmental Dictatorship,* pp. 206–13.

housing facilities, and health care were improved. The Labor Charter was considered an advance in protective legislation. Maternity and child care, pension, and old-age support were instituted, and insurance, road work, and other programs were begun. Mussolini instituted reforms in demographic policy. According to some authors, the emigration and colonial policies were tied to this; certainly, war and colonialism provided a demographic outlet.[26] According to some fascist authors, expansionism was the ultimate solution. In this way, Fascist economic, demographic, and colonial policies converged.

Noninstitutionalized Praetorian and Corporatist Authoritarianism

Noninstitutionalized authoritarian systems are distinguished from their institutionalized counterparts by a conspicuous absence or ineffectiveness of the parallel and auxiliary structures that are instruments of political mobilization and control. But noninstitutionalized authoritarian systems use parallel structures for the purpose of control rather than for mobilization. These systems, not strongly committed to economic mobilization, are strongly committed to the drive for power. Noninstitutionalized authoritarian regimes generally rule by executive, politically restricted power; but such power, though restricted, is not exclusive. The less complex the political system, the more effective executive control will be; this is the rationale for restricted power. Exclusivity refers to exclusive rule over the oligopolistic structures of power by a political elite to ensure it will retain control while it mobilizes social forces. Institutionalized authoritarian systems are political and economic mobilizational specialists; this is not true of noninstitutionalized authoritarian systems.

Political Dynamics. Oligarchy is at the heart of exclusionary corporatist and praetorian politics. The regimes substitute patrimonial, oligarchic, bureaucratic, or corporate arrangements for an otherwise institutionalized party-state or state-dominated au-

26. Renzo De Felice, *The Interpretations of Fascism* (Cambridge, Mass.: Harvard University Press, 1977).

thoritarianism. Thus, praetorian regimes restrict political mobilization and seek political support from national, but only partly institutionalized, structures—corporate coalitions of the military, the church, labor unions, and industrialists—on a patrimonial and clientalistic basis.

In sub-Saharan Africa we have witnessed the rise of a number of praetorian tyrannies: Uganda, the Central African Republic, Zaire, Chad, and Togo. In each we have seen the emergence of a tyrant whose chief concern is to stay in power and is thus motivated to annihilate any opposition, whether within or outside of the military. Decalo's model states that some African armies are noncohesive, tribal, non-Westernized, nonprofessional, and personalist; they are as corrupt and inefficient as the civilian regimes they have replaced. Recruitment and promotion are based not on skill or merit, but on personal idiosyncrasies or on the tyrant's tribal connections. The military is neither interested in nor capable of increasing the momentum of modernization and mobilization. Grievances are not corporate but personalist; competing ambitions are of greater import than so-called national aspirations.[27]

The typical praetorian oligarchy in the Middle East has been hailed by some authors as a military-populist regime that rules a mass political party. Nothing could be further from the truth: Nasser's three attempts to build a political party based on the army demonstrate that he was opposed to a cadre party. Furthermore, he never could decide whether the Arab Socialist Union (ASU) should be a populist party. In fact, the ASU (as well as the Ba'ath party, which is dominated by the Syrian and Iraqi military) is actually an auxiliary instrument of the military oligarchy. The Egyptian system of rule was and continues to be patrimonial, repressive, and unstructured.[28]

Syria since 1970 clearly illustrates the characteristics of a praetorian and patrimonial oligarchy.[29] The oligarchic system

27. Samuel Decalo, *Military Rule in Africa* (New Haven: Yale University Press, 1976), pp. 14–15.
28. Perlmutter, *Egypt: The Praetorian State* (New Brunswick, N.J.: Transaction, 1974).
29. A. I. Dawisha, "Syria under Assad 1970–1978," in *Government and Opposition* 13 (Summer 1978): 341–54.

evolved with three decision-making structures—the party, the presidency and the defense establishment. The presidency is controlled by the former chief of the air force, President Assad, who dominates the Ba'ath party and the military establishment. Asad's authority stems from societal factors and, more importantly, from his oligarchical-praetorian alliance with the Ba'ath party and with the military.

The president, especially in national security matters, consults with both the minister of defense and the chief of staff. Both the president and the military are ideologically and personally affiliated with the Ba'ath party, whose influence with the presidency stems from this praetorian and oligarchic system. The president, who has a role in all three structures, enhances the institutional oligarchic domination. The national leadership of the party is an institutional oligarchy composed of President Asad, members of the military, and the national cabinet, in which the military predominates as it does in the party itself. The propensity of the military to intervene in both party and national politics typifies the dynamics of this type of praetorianism.[30]

The case that dependency represents the major obstacle to development has been the cause célèbre of third world intellectuals and liberal analysts. Unquestionably, the politics of contemporary Egypt, Peru, Cuba, and Bolivia could not be explained if the legacy of dependency were not emphasized. Egypt's efforts to overcome its economic and social dependency illustrate the problems inherent in dependency and its role in obstructing development.[31] Egypt did experiment with all three of the models of economic development prevailing since 1945: a gradualist state-capitalist model between 1956 and 1961; a state socialist model between 1962 and 1967; and oligarchic capitalism from 1971 to the present. In all three instances, the etatist, patrimonial, and authoritarian orientations prevailed; the models were accompanied by praetorian and

30. Ibid., pp. 343, 350.
31. Vatikiotis, *Nasser and His Generation* (London: Croom Helm, 1978), pp. 201–24; Patrick O'Brien, *The Revolution of Egypt's Economic System* (London: Oxford University Press, 1966); Perlmutter, *Egypt: The Praetorian State;* and R. Dekmedjian, *Egypt Under Nasir: A Study in Political Dynamics* (Albany: State University of New York Press, 1971).

oligarchic orientations and practices. The struggle between the
Arab Socialist Union and the military, which the latter won, was
over political power, not over the socialist economic model espoused by the ASU.[32]

In Egypt, "real power . . . did not flow through the officially pre-
scribed constitutional channels. Crucial to the actual system of rule
was the relationship established by Nasser between his regime and
the military establishment."[33] Thus Nasser and Sadat have governed by the power of executive authoritarianism, supported by
patrimonial relationships. The executive of these two praetorians
has been a patrimonial kaleidoscope, especially during the regime
of Sadat. The people recruited into the most intimate structure of
power—the presidential office—came from the patrimonial network of family, village, and kinship relationships. The bureaucracy
and the military were also feudal patrimonies composed of rela-
tives; loyalists in the military; the police; the single party; the parliament; the press; the governments of Cairo, Alexandria, and the
twenty-four provinces; and professors, lawyers, engineers, and
physicians.

To reiterate Raymond Baker, the connection between the state
and the feudalization of power created two serious problems: a
struggle between the old and the new oligarchies and a "critical
personalization of power."[34] Power was derived from the patrimonial system, whose highest political value was a personal loyalty to
the Rais. Both Nasser and Sadat were ambivalent about the military, although both were military conspirators whose power depended solely on the military's loyalty. Both, especially Sadat, destroyed military sources of power when they could: Nasser tried
and failed to do so after 1967.[35] Sadat purged his senior military
three times (1971, 1973, and 1978); yet each time he made sure that

32. John Waterbury, "Egypt: The Wages of Dependency," in The Middle
East: Oil, Conflict and Hope, ed. A. L. Udovich (Lexington: University of
Massachusetts Press, 1976), pp. 291–351; and Raymond W. Baker, Egypt's
Uncertain Revolution Under Sadat and Nasser (Cambridge, Mass.: Harvard
University Press, 1978), pp. 44–114.
33. Baker, Egypt's Uncertain Revolution, p. 81.
34. Ibid., pp. 80–81.
35. Ibid., pp. 94–114.

each outgoing military officer would be replaced by another praetorian. Thus, in an effort to professionalize and depoliticize the military, Nasser and Sadat used it against itself, a practice which is explained by the need to pay lip service to mass and party political solutions. In fact, it was done to enhance the power of the supreme praetorian. The ASU, Nasser's answer to the political challenge of a society in transition, ended as another appendage to the elephantine Egyptian bureaucracy.[36]

The existence of a praetorian oligarchy nevertheless explains the dynamics of Egypt's uncertain revolution from Nasser to Sadat. "In the Egypt of Sadat, as of Nasser," writes Baker, "real power rested with the military/police complex, not with civilian institutions. If anything, Sadat only enhances the power and prestige of Egypt's officer corps."[37]

The patrimonial-praetorian autocracy governs in the doldrums between a classical patrimonial regime and modern institutionalized patrimonialism which encompasses the state, the presidency, the police, the military, the party, the press, and the parliament. The military/police dualism represents the dynamics of praetorianism. The individuals chosen to head these structures are clients who oversee the praetorian state on behalf of the patrimony. The relationships of authority, and thus the political dynamics, are patrimonial and personalist in praetorian Syria and Iraq as well as in Egypt.

In Latin America, corporate and praetorian authoritarianism is connected with the region's previous pattern of economic development. Malloy calls it delayed dependent development (DDD), which is a combination of a lag in the initiation of economic development and dependency on the United States. Populism is the first response to DDD. During the 1930s and 1940s, a highly bureaucratized and largely dependent middle class produced various new formulations of populism: the Alianza Popular Revolucionaria Americana (APRA) in Peru, Acción Democrática in Venezuela, Peronismo in Argentina, and the Movimiento Nacional

36. See Perlmutter, *Egypt: The Praetorian State*, pp. 157–99; and Baker, *Egypt's Revolution*, pp. 108–113.
37. Baker, *Egypt's Uncertain Revolution*, p. 158.

Revolucionaria in Bolivia. Some of these populist movements were
statist, corporatist, and authoritarian.[38]

The 1960s brought a new structural crisis. Acting under the
guise of protecting national security and advancing national development, blatantly authoritarian and corporatist alliances of
soldiers and technocrats emerged, first in Brazil in 1964, then in
Argentina (1966), Peru (1968), and finally in Chile (1973). Exclusionary politics, except in the case of Peru, restricted mobilization, and the growth of corporatist conglomerates and
state bureaucracies did not strengthen the state, the regime, or the
society. Instead, it benefited only the patrons of the corporatist
groups whose client, the state, reversed its historical role in civil-
military relations. The soldier became the state's chief patron.[39]

Populist authoritarianism promoted by Perón, Goulart, and
Vargas gave an impetus to the rise of mass mobilizational systems.
Both internal and external structural economic constraints im-
peded sustained economic growth in Latin American societies. Delayed development was thwarted by dependency, and the rapid increase of the people's economic demands on governments led to
praetorianism and overbureaucratization. This dependence was
characterized by direct US private investment, foreign debt, and
extensive trade with the United States.[40]

Under corporate praetorianism, the dictatorship shares power
with a coalition of political bureaucrats and technocrats; under
praetorian oligarchy, power is shared with the bureaucrats,
technocrats, and former loyal army officers. The tyrannical military regime refuses to share power, exerting control through fear
and assassination. The most interesting fact about corporate and
praetorian regimes is that *all* have emerged during periods when
weak political systems (whether monarchical, imperial, republican, or parliamentary) were being replaced. The praetorians, how-

38. James Malloy, ed., *Authoritarianism and Corporatism in Latin
America* (Pittsburgh: Pittsburgh University Press, 1977), pp. 4–9, 15.

39. For pertinent literature, see Steffen Schmidt et al., eds., *Friends,
Followers, and Factions* (Berkeley: University of California Press, 1977), es-
says by Carl Lande, John Powell, Eric Wolfe, Douglas Chalmers, and Lily
Taylor.

40. D. Palmer, "The Politics" in *Authoritarianism,* ed. James Malloy, pp.
384–89.

ever, could not handle the demands of modern politics; for example, they could not create a viable political system in the old colonial territories.

A continuous, unresolved controversy between political leaders of praetorian tyrannies and their opponents is whether these regimes have achieved more than nonpraetorian regimes in political development, economic modernization, and social change. There is little doubt that they have provided the symbols of newly acquired nationhood for their people. Nevertheless, there is a consensus among social scientists and historians that praetorian regimes, on the whole, are unstable and noninstitutionalized and that they restrict political mobilization. There is no consensus on the dynamics of economic modernization and its relationship to politics and ideology in corporate-praetorian autocracies.[41]

Economic Dynamics. Oligarchic and corporate praetorian states seek to establish some type of modern economic system. However, they have no consistent economic orientation or policy; one usually finds them employing a mixture of socialism, state capitalism, and atavistic economics. Emphasis on growth and technocratic skills is prominent in the most advanced corporate praetorian regimes (Brazil, Argentina, Chile, and Peru, for example).

O'Donnell and Malloy both argue that the emergence of bureaucratic authoritarianism and praetorianism in Brazil and Argentina since the middle 1960s was directly linked to policies aimed at excluding the popular sector.[42] O'Donnell traces the ori-

41. For a summary of the controversy, see Amos Perlmutter, *The Military and Politics in Modern Times* (New Haven: Yale University Press, 1977), preface, chaps. 4, 5. In defense of oligarchic praetorianism, see John J. Johnson, ed., *The Role of the Military in Underdeveloped Countries* (Princeton, N.J.: Princeton University Press, 1962); and Morris Janowitz, *The Military in the Political Development of New Nations* (Chicago: University of Chicago, 1964). Opposing views are presented in S. P. Huntington, "Political Development and Political Decay," *World Politics* 18 (April 1965): 386–430; and Amos Perlmutter, "The Arab Military Elite," *World Politics* 22 (January 1970): 269–300.

42. Guillermo O'Donnell, *Modernization and Bureaucratic Authoritarianism* (Berkeley: Institute of International Studies, 1973), pp. 79, 90–92.

gins of these regimes to the modernization and urbanization revolution. A high level of modernization, O'Donnell argues, increases the gap between the society and the state. It pushes the regime toward praetorianism by forging a coalition, which is authoritarian and coercive, between the technocracy, the military and the middle class.[43] In Brazil, the use of coercion excluded and deactivated the popular sector; the same eventually occurred in Argentina and Chile. Governments cannot count on the support of sectors other than that of the technocrats, and economic development requires a low level of social unrest.[44] Thus, the high level of modernization in Brazil, Argentina, Chile, and Peru stimulated authoritarianism, corporatism, and praetorianism.

I object to O'Donnell's description of Brazil, Argentina, and Chile during the 1970s as post-praetorian regimes. Bureaucratic authoritarianism and corporatism do not exclude praetorianism; they enhance it. O'Donnell himself characterizes the bureaucratic authoritarian model as identified with a high level of modernization. This is also true of modern authoritarianism: the bureaucratic authoritarian model represents a phase of exclusionary corporate praetorianism, not a post-praetorian regime.

Consider the case of Nasser's Egypt. Baker's perceptive conclusion should be quoted at length.

> Faced with the task of developing Egypt increasingly in terms of its own resources, Nasser realized that he had not created the political tools—neither the ideology nor the organized and motivated cadres—that would be necessary. More damaging still was the realization that the political system shaped under Nasser's aegis worked actively against the creation of these tools. The nonparticipation of the masses, the isolation of the intellectuals, the prominence of bureaucratic and military figures, with the resultant ascendancy of bureaucratic methods and inflation of defense spending, and above all the channelling of political energies into personalized struggles for power, characterized that system. The impact of these flaws was crip-

43. Ibid., p. 101.
44. Ibid., pp. 106–07.

pling to Nasser's efforts in the mid-sixties to build a political party and fashion an ideology geared to the demands of transforming Egypt through a strategy involving mass participation. Such a "political solution" had to be abandoned.[45]

What an epitaph for praetorianism! And Nasser's Egypt, despite its limited modernization, is an ideal example of bureaucratic authoritarianism. When a military regime initiates a social revolution, it nevertheless remains praetorian and authoritarian. If Egypt is an indication, it also fails to realize development.

Social Dynamics. In the absence of a strong party, state, or other permanent political structures, and where there is no economic diversity, social classes cannot be expected to cluster within party or state auxiliaries as they did in the bolshevik or nazi systems. Apparatchiks are insignificant in number and the civil service is impotent under corporatist praetorian regimes. The social system is atomized and is dominated by a few scattered political and economic classes. Praetorian systems are neither class nor mass societies. Their political structures have few or no stable social and economic foundations. Nevertheless, the oligarchic and corporatist praetorian regimes with developed economics encourage and support the growth of middle classes and sometimes of skilled working classes.

In Egypt, Nasser encouraged the emergence of military bureaucratic effendis while Sadat brought back the bankers and the pashas. Institutional instability does not encourage the ascendence of any classes other than the bureaucratic-technocratic allies of the regime. In Chile and Argentina, all potential rivals are brutally repressed.

The regime becomes the arbiter of class conflict. This was true in Nasser's Egypt, which repressed the middle classes, and in Sadat's, which does the same to the bureaucratic socialists. In Syria and Iraq, the radical military oligarchy tolerates no classes but is impotent to suppress everyone, including its own class and the military in general. In tyrannical praetorian regimes, assassi-

45. Baker, *Egypt's Uncertain Revolution*, p. 237.

nation of the opposition has removed marginal social classes or groups from politics.[46]

Authoritarianism and Development in Noninstitutionalized Systems: The Argument

With the exception of Nazi Germany, all modern authoritarian regimes have been established in economically underdeveloped societies that were in the process of replacing politically unstable regimes. Authoritarianism thrives in societies whose development has been thwarted and where the natural evolution of political and economic structures characteristic of developed societies has failed to materialize. But underdevelopment encompasses more than economic backwardness, for authoritarianism also thrives in societies that are relatively developed economically (the USSR, Fascist Italy, Brazil, Argentina, Chile, for example), highly developed (such as Nazi Germany), and in state capitalist societies (such as prewar Japan and contemporary South Korea and Taiwan). Furthermore, the USSR and certainly East Germany are no longer economically underdeveloped states. They are developmental authoritarian systems; the successful developmental and mobilizational efforts, however, enhanced, helped to institutionalize, and even legitimized authoritarian political institutions, structures and procedures.

On the other hand, not all economically backward societies are governed by developmentally oriented authoritarian regimes. Patrimonial and nonmodern regimes, typified by several of the Latin American and Persian Gulf societies (including Iran under the Pahlavis and the Ayatollah) are governed by traditional authoritaian regimes which are not oriented toward either mass mobilization or economic and political development.

Among modern authoritarian political systems I have distinguished between two types: politically developed and polit-

46. For the argument for the nonmobilizational, nondevelopmental nature of praetorian-oligarchic regimes, see Huntington, "Political Development"; Perlmutter, *Military and Politics in Modern Times;* and Decalo, *Military Rule in Africa.*

ically underdeveloped regimes. Development normally refers to socioeconomic changes and the formation of modern productive systems, or industrialization.[47] When I speak of development, I mean a comprehensive process of change that goes with and beyond socioeconomic development. Development means modernization, secularization, urbanization, technicalization, and deparochialization of politics and values.[48] Only communism, and to a great extent fascism, fully responded to the developmental revolution, though they chose alternative methods of mobilization. "Both were reactive national response to relative developmental retardation."[49] Both, because of their comprehensive approaches toward development, complemented this aspiration with the creation of tightly controlled, centralized political structures, which enabled them to implement their developmental programs. To increase the regulative and extractive capabilities of a central state, fascist and communist regimes established comprehensive political-structural and institutional networks.[50] To extract maximum human and labor resources, developmental authoritarianism totally politicized the central state and expanded the police and the party. Thus, it is clear that highly institutionalized authoritarianism is correlated with powerful, ambitious, and fiercely competing structures that are parts of the central state, the government, the military, and the party and are aimed at mass mobilization, coercion, control, and legitimation. The irony is that, contrary to theorists' predictions in the 1950s and 1960s, political institutionalization and development led to the strengthening not of democratic regimes, but of authoritarian ones. Only authoritarian regimes have been successful in creating political institutions that can mobilize society while controlling it and in channelling demands to the central decision-making structure.

47. See discussion in Gregor, *Italian Fascism and Developmental Dictatorship*, pp. 491–95.
48. For a complete list of mobilization indicators, see John W. Hall, "Changing Attitudes toward Modernization of Japan," in *Changing Japanese Attitudes toward Modernization*, ed. Marius B. Jansen (Princeton, N.J.: Princeton University Press), pp. 1–41.
49. Gregor, *Italian Fascism and Developmental Dictatorship*, p. 303.
50. Ibid., pp. 304–305.

The developmental model, as I define it, is mainly an effort to establish a more durable and effective *political* authority. I distinguish between political *development* and economic *modernization*. At least in the third world, the developmental model has been associated with nationalist anticolonialism more than with economic theories.

Nevertheless, economic underdevelopment is not a politically neutral concept. Developmentalism, whether in state socialist or state capitalist societies, also means the motivation on the part of a regime, a party, or an oligarchy to change objective conditions. Politically, it is the desire to become modern in all of its aspects: political, economic, and social. In that sense, Nazi Germany could be excluded. Hitler did not make the country modern; he only turned Germany into an authoritarian state since it already had one of the world's most modern and efficient economic systems. But in many modern authoritarian regimes developmentalism and authoritarianism are closely linked, and one could not be fulfilled without the other. Post-Hitler Germany succeeded in remaining modern and becoming democratic. As yet, none of the examples of modernizing authoritarianism have turned away from authoritarianism. Political elites in modern authoritarian states have no reason to adopt nonauthoritarian political structures and practices in order to resolve their state and economic backwardness and political underdevelopment.

In this sense, economic development is deeply linked to the modern authoritarian system. In fact, the functions of authoritarian political structures are often closely connected to aspirations to change unsatisfactory economic conditions. Economic development and authoritarian political structures are symbiotic in many authoritarian political systems.

However, most noninstitutionalized praetorian states have not created the powerful political institutions that can implement an economic development program. In the populist, corporatist, and praetorian states, the developmental revolution is usually no more than the rhetoric of charismatic and populist leaders who have created political structures largely to protect personal and tyrannical rule. Their populist images notwithstanding, Nasser, Nkrumah, and Sukarno established few or no political or economic developmental structures aimed at mass mobilization. In fact, neither the Portuguese corporatist state nor oligarchic praetorian states like Egypt, Syria, or Iraq have created viable, working instruments for mass mobilization.

Even in those countries that have some success in their development efforts and in which regimes come to power in response to economic crises whether latent or actual, the priority is given to political development over economic development.

In most authoritarian political systems, the political structures are modern and new, and the auxiliary and parallel structures are revolutionary. The same cannot be said of most of the economic structures in noninstitutionalized authoritarian systems. In fact, the energy, commitment, and effort that the elites devote to the furthering of the state's political control is greater on the whole than their interest in creating new economic structures. Even when they do devote their attention to economic modernization, their first priority is still the defense of oligopolistic political structures, and not the successful operation and maintenance of these economic structures. The differences between institutionalized and praetorian systems are based on their attitudes toward economic development. Institutionalized systems achieve a balance between political structures for control and economic institutions for development. Praetorian systems abandon economic development if it seriously threatens the political instruments of control.

The true developmental regimes are complex, all-inclusive, and revolutionary. This is true of the USSR, China, Cuba, the Koreas, and Taiwan. The modernizing regimes, on the other hand, are not necessarily developmental; they are usually restrictive (for example, Nasser's Egypt and Peru in the period 1968–73) in the sense that not all of the political structures or major classes participate in the developmental revolution. Autocracies like Egypt, Syria, Iraq, Peru, and Ecuador, have restricted the developmental role to primarily military institutions and elites; some of the military's bureaucratic and political allies are also included in the modernization process in order to enhance its political power. These regimes dominate a nonparticipatory peasantry. None of these reformist autocracies has been successful in mobilizing the peasantry. Although Nasser in Egypt and the military reformers in

160 AUTHORITARIANISM AND DEVELOPMENT

Peru attempted it, their efforts foundered. Only the communist
model succeeded in mobilizing the peasantry even though peasants
are not prominent among the Soviet, Chinese, and Cuban elites; the
urban-oriented intelligentsia, the military, and the bureaucracy
still command the peasant revolutions in these countries. Thus, development, however secular, is a restrictive, structured elitist system.

While the political structures in developmental systems are inclusionary, their elites, especially if the military predominates, are
exclusionary. The political structures are modernized to accommodate and mobilize "pluralistic" elites. The scope of elite domination in modernizing military regimes can vary. In Iraq, the
modernizing group is the Ba'ath party elite. In Syria, the military
elite is the modernizing group. The modernizing groups in both
countries represent economic and group interests, but they are not
developmental authoritarian regimes. In China and Cuba, the military as an institution is a most important agent of modernization,
but at the present it is only an ally—sometimes passive, sometimes
active—of the developmental revolution that is dominated by
symbiotic party-army elites. I know of no military elite, except for
that of Cuba and possibly of communist Vietnam, that has succeeded in creating a developmental system equal to those of China,
the USSR, and Fascist Italy in its ability to mobilize peasants and
workers. The state capitalist developmental systems of prewar
Japan and postwar South Korea and Taiwan, which were dominated by the state-oriented capitalist class, also succeeded in
mobilizing the peasantry and the workers. These capitalist developmental systems modernized as well. Communism, socialism,
and reformism have no monopoly over successful developmental
and modernizing regimes. Both developmentalism and modernization are essentially collectivist societal goals and actions; but
neither rightist nor leftist ideology has a monopoly over the political processes of modernizing authoritarian regimes.

Turning to the communist model, some students of the post-
Stalinist USSR audaciously, though unconvincingly, have tried to
demonstrate that the next stage of communism will take the form
of diffused, institutionalized authoritarianism, which would entail
the formation of limited interest group politics and of institutional

pluralism in the USSR. Authoritarianism, even when linked to political institutional and economic development, does not guarantee pluralism, democratization, or greater social justice. It only assures elite integration at the center and post-Stalinist pacification of the institutionalized Soviet elites, especially the military. Development promotes the stabilization of authoritarianism, not limited pluralism. The more complex authoritarian systems are not simple historical or personal tyrannies. Yet the confusion that stems from misinterpretation of complex economic and political systems (authoritarian or democratic) as pluralist, leads several authors (Linz on Latin America; Hough, Skilling, and others on the USSR) to assume that economic decentralization and functional diversification enhance some type of pluralist and clandestinely implied liberalism. This is a misapplication of the concept. At the center, where politics and policy initiatives meet, the system is authoritarian. The diffusion of authoritarian structures and institutions creates a more stable authoritarian system, a more satisfied and competitive elite, greater efficiency, and more control over public and consumer needs.

Institutionalized pluralism, which occurred in Latin America in the 1950s and 1960s, refers to the creation of elite consensus, not greater democracy. In our context, institutionalized pluralism means more effective and integrated authoritarianism with increased party-army symbiosis, as the USSR, China, Vietnam, and Cuba exemplify.

The social reality of the USSR, Brazil, Argentina, and even Egypt is that the initiation and implementation of important policy are conducted in a completely authoritarian atmosphere. The limited pluralism model obscures rather than clarifies the dynamics of authoritarian systems because it is a conceptual tool that supposedly distinguishes authoritarianism from totalitarianism.[51] Unquestionably, providing an economic and structural

51. Jerry Hough is the chief advocate of the diffusion of authoritarian power in the USSR and the innovator of the institutional pluralism model. See Jerry Hough, *The Soviet Union and Social Science Theory* (Cambridge, Mass.: Harvard University Press, 1977), pp. 1–108. A pioneer effort to apply the concepts of interest groups to the bolshevik model is found in H. Gordon Skilling and Franklyn Griffiths, *Interest Groups in Soviet Politics* (Princeton,

solution for development is the end goal of modern authoritarian regimes. These regimes are characterized by innovative political and structural development. They are not the most advanced models of economic development, but they do represent the most advanced forms of authoritarian structure and behavior. In fact, in several authoritarian regimes the top leadership spends more time and money and uses its influence and coercion more extensively to promote the formation of political structures than to support large-scale economic development. Certainly, the two decades of Stalin's authoritarianism and political institution building far surpassed his concern with economic developmental projects. Stalin destroyed the party, strengthened the police, annihilated the officer corps, established gulags, destroyed the peasantry, and created a system of forced labor. It is, certainly, one model for development. I make no moral judgement; I simply record the fact that Stalin's system succeeded not because of its developmental orientations but because of its political authoritarianism, which modernized the USSR. The police and their role in the permanent purge of leaders, peoples, and Bolshevik structures were designed to institutionalize the Stalinist modernizing tyranny, not to develop the economy. Stalin's barbarism did change the economic structure of the USSR, but the party and ideology were not the vehicles of Stalin's authoritariansim as they would be in Linz's ideal totalitarian state. On the contrary, the instruments that, according to some theorists, should be used to achieve a totalitarian state were subjugated to Stalin's personal authority.[52]

Mussolini's efforts to institutionalize the corporate state were also guided by political rather than economic developmental orientations. The grand debate over the developmental motivations of modern authoritarian regimes is replete with arguments

N.J.: Princeton University Press, 1971). See also William Odom, "A Dissenting View of the Group Theory Approach to Soviet Politics," *World Politics* 25 (July 1976): 542–67; and Sidney Ploss, "New Politics in Russia," *Survey* 19, no. 1 (1973): 23–35.

52. See S. P. Huntington, "Paradigms of American Politics: Beyond the One, the Two and the Many," *Political Science Quarterly* 89 (March 1974): 12. See also Odom, "Dissenting View," pp. 544–45, 566–67.

as to whether fascism and corporatist praetorianism sincerely tackled economic underdevelopment and whether the mass mobilizational efforts of authoritarian regimes in underdeveloped societies were directed toward truly mobilizing or harnessing the masses. Developmental mobilization came in response to a combination of retarded industrial development, latent nationalist unification, and the absence of governmental authority and political order. Economic backwardness and the lack of a developmental posture are insufficient to explain the emergence of modern authoritarianism.[53] On the other hand, limited pluralism cannot explain authoritarianism's demise.

Corporatist and praetorian regimes have been more efficient in transferring power than in managing the socioeconomic changes necessary to fulfill developmental aspirations. Under communist regimes, the developmental model presented a challenge to the transfer of power. In order to ensure the stability of the revolutionary order, authoritarian political structures and behavior were established and inculcated into society. With a link between the source of authority and the people, a successful combination of authoritarian structures and economic institutions would result in a stable order. Once again, one should not confuse economic development with developmental mobilization systems. The economic development of oligarchic praetorianism is impressive if compared with the lethargy and backwardness of past regimes in some states. Yet to my mind, neither Nasserism in the Arab Middle East nor Nkrumahism in sub-Saharan Africa was dedicated to establishing mass developmental or mobilization systems. The strategy of development in Egypt under Nasser was linked to

53. For a defense of the thesis that fascism is a mass mobilizing modernizing model, see A. James Gregor, *The Fascist Persuasion in Radical Politics* (Princeton, N.J.: Princeton University Press, 1974), pp. 303–34; and Gregor, *Italian Fascism and Developmental Dictatorship.* See also, A. James Gregor, "Fascism and Modernization: Some Addenda," *World Politics* 26 (April 1974): 370–84; and A. James Gregor, "Renzo De Felice and the Fascist Phenomenon," *World Politics* 24 (July 1972): 547–64. See also A. F. K. Organski, *The Stages of Political Development* (New York: Knopf, 1965); and A. F. K. Organski, "Fascism and Modernization," in *The Nature of Fascism,* ed. S. J. Woolf (New York: Random House, 1969).

populist politics and to the maintenance of a regime enforced by
the Nasserite Free Officers. Nkrumah exploited the mass party in
order to institutionalize his personal tyranny, again at the expense
of both political and economic development.

In the case of Latin American praetorian and corporatist systems, innovative political development was designed to harness
mass movements. This was especially true in corporatist regimes in
Latin America, but the emphasis placed by them on economic ra-
tionality and development and technocracy should not be confused
with developmentalism. These regimes only seek developmental
programs that will not threaten the regime's authority. In fact, the
original corporatist state was inaugurated as an alternative to
mass mobilization in an age of modernization.[54]

The only institutionalized authoritarian regime not dedicated
to the developmental model was Nazi Germany. It is significant
that it became the archetypal police state because the police state
is the most efficient type of authoritarian, but not developmental,
state. However, the Nazis did not hinder economic development
and industrialization. On the contrary, Hitler's war ambitions led
to the full exploitation of Germany's industrial might for military
purposes. Neither a developmental nor a mass mobilizational regime, the Nazi state, not the Nazi party, exploited the resources
of the German society. Though not always successful, Hitler harnessed the state and the party machinery to the fulfillment of his
personal imperialistic ambitions and not developmental processes.
A developmental model would not be of great use to explain the
political behavior of nazi authoritarianism.

In praetorian regimes, modernization is not oriented toward
fostering justice, equality, and a better life, as it is in developmental revolutionary political systems. To make a moral distinction
between exploiting the lower classes and excluding them by distinguishing between inclusionary and exclusionary corporatist regimes is a valid political and ethical argument. Politically, however,
both types of regimes, whether populist or bureaucratic, are au-

54. Susan Kaufman Purcell, *The Mexican Profit-Sharing Decision* (Berkeley: University of California Press, 1975), pp. 1–11.

thoritarian, inasmuch as they have exclusive executives, docile legislatures, nonautonomous interest groups, weak or nonexistent party systems, low levels of participation, and a clientalistic, dependent style of rulership.[55]

The distinction between the nature of the authoritarian executive in revolutionary and in praetorian regimes is important, In the latter, the executive lacks elite integration, cohesion, and cooperation, while in the former the opposite is the case.

The difference between revolutionary (communist, nazi, fascist) and corporatist and praetorian systems goes deeper. The crucial distinction is found in their orientations toward developmentalism. In praetorian, noninstitutionalized regimes, the attitude toward developmentalism is reactive and defensive; in revolutionary, institutionalized authoritarian regimes, the developmental drive is aggressive, all-inclusive, and progressive. The similarity between institutionalized and praetorian regimes lies in their political-structural and institutional arrangements. Even though the size, scope, level, degree of cohesion, and efficiency differ, once more, political structures of modern authoritarianism have been *designed* to harness and enhance the developmental revolution: to encourage it while maintaining strict control over it. Thus, orientations toward modernization, urbanization, and other variables that portend socioeconomic change suggest a dedication not to developmentalism alone, but to authoritarianism as a system of governing. In fact, modernization can, and in several nonrevolutionary and noninstitutionalized praetorian and corporate systems does, foster and strengthen defensive and developmentally arresting practices. In these cases, the politics of modernization are also the politics of arresting the developmental revolution or of building up and sustaining authoritarian political structures. The success of communism is expressed in a stable political order. The failure of Nasserism is expressed in Egypt's unstable political system. In the former case, once the authoritarian structures were in-

55. Purcell, *The Mexican Profit-Sharing Decision* is an excellent study demonstrating their problems. I take strong issue with her, however, when she writes that a nonintegrative unstable praetorian state is not authoritarian (p. 7). This is not in conformity with her own definition (p. 12, pp. 3–5).

stitutionalized, the regime became more successful in implementing developmental programs. Nasser's Egypt failed to establish political legitimacy and economic development.

Kenneth Erickson discusses the attitudes toward developmentalism and political participation of two different praetorian regimes in Brazil.[56] Using the ministry of labor as a case study for the analysis of corporatist authoritarian regimes, Erickson delineates the attitudes toward labor policy of, respectively, the bureaucratic regime (1964 to present), which was reactive and restrictive, and João Goulart's regime from 1961 to 1964, which maintained a populist policy toward lower class participation. Both regimes were "organized and led by politicians from the ruling class."[57] Goulart's regime emphasized economic nationalism, state enterprises, and equitable distribution of goods and services, while the bureaucratic regime emphasized a developmental or modernization program that strengthened the middle class. Erickson's data clearly demonstrate that in the bureaucratic regime the benefits of development were captured by the administrative class, which restricted the "scope of political conflict" and excluded the workers.[58] While the populist, radical regime improved the conditions of the workers, it nevertheless failed to change the power structure.[59] In my view, this failure occurred because praetorian regimes, however radical and popular, are restrictive, noninstitutionalized, and nonintegrative. The failure was that of the corporatist system, not of the different ideological orientations.

As Erickson shows, under different (nonpraetorian) conditions, developmentalism can revolutionize the social as well as the political system. Corporatist systems do not lend themselves to revolutionary change even under the most propitious conditions of modernization and development. Erickson concludes, "the civil-military coalition which took power in 1964 replaced the populist system with an authoritarian, technocratic policy. The new rulers,

56. Kenneth Erickson, *The Brazilian Corporative State and Working-Class Politics* (Berkeley: University of California Press, 1977), chap. 4, pp. 49–76.
57. Ibid., p. 49.
58. Ibid., pp. 75–76.
59. Ibid., pp. 90–91.

their political control bolstered by repression and their economic position strengthened by vast investment sums from foreign sources, applied technocratic measures to bring union militancy and strike activity under control."[60]

The regime that has controlled Peru since 1968 is not precisely analogous structurally to those of Argentina, Brazil or Chile. Nevertheless, under both Velasco and Bermudez, Peru's regime has been corporatist, praetorian, and authoritarian.[61] Once again, Peru represents the failure of the corporatist model. Both Velasco's and Bermudez's regimes demonstrate the corporatist system's impotence to bring about modernization and reform and to establish authority. As Collier demonstrated, reform calls for the existence of autonomous social-political groups. These groups may have existed in Chile from 1970 to 1973 but their presence in Peru has not been demonstrated.[62] Between 1968 and 1975, Peru had a reformist regime.[63] Velasco and his military government went beyond some observers' expectations and transformed the basic structures of Peru's economy and politics—this process is irreversible—yet the reform and the reformers failed.[64] Its central features were self-management, worker participation, and industrial democracy—Stepan's inclusionary corporatism. Velasco implemented a radical agrarian reform (which Nasser, for example, never did) and developed self-management institutions, especially in the agrarian sectors. Yet he failed to win popular support and

60. Ibid., p. 173.
61. See Abraham Lowenthal, *The Peruvian Experiment* (Princeton, N.J.: Princeton University Press, 1975); Kevin Middlebrook and David Palmer, *Military Government and Political Development: Lessons from Peru* (Los Angeles: Sage, 1975); Cynthia McClintock, *Self-Management and Political Participation in Peru, 1969–1975: The Corporate Illusion* (Los Angeles: Sage, 1975); David Collier, *Squatters and Oligarchs* (Baltimore: Johns Hopkins University Press, 1976).
62. Collier, *Squatters and Oligarchs*, p. 133.
63. Cynthia McClintock, "The Ambiguity of Peru's Third Way: Costs and Benefits" (Paper delivered at Wilson Center workshop on "The Peruvian Experiment Reconsidered," Washington, D.C., November 2–4, 1978); and Peter Cleaves, "A Decade of Military Policymaking in Peru, 1968–1978" (Paper delivered at Wilson Center workshop on "The Peruvian Experiment Reconsidered," Washington, D.C., November 2–4, 1978).
64. McClintock, "The Ambiguity of Peru's Third Way."

the government's ultimate intentions were ambiguous. The autonomy of the military was established at the expense not only of the oligarchy but also of the very group which the regime tried to create, liberate, and incorporate: the lower classes.

As I have argued earlier, in noninstitutionalized authoritarian regimes cohesive, collective behavior is largely absent. By definition, the praetorian military is authoritarian, bureaucratic (not in O'Donnell's limited sense), and impotent to organize socioeconomic structures and groups. In fact, it is unable to establish viable political systems even of the corporatist type. For example, McClintock has demonstrated that in Peru corporatism exists, if at all, only on organizational charts. The same is true of the Portuguese and Brazilian regimes, which had corporatist orientations but whose corporatist systems soon collapsed. In the case of Peru, Stepan clearly demonstrated that the problems of policy implementation once more are connected with the nature of the political structures and institutions. The reformist regime of 1968–75 failed because it never institutionalized itself.[65] It did not consolidate new political patterns of succession, control and participation, it mismanaged the economic reform system, it failed to recruit more stable constituencies to support the reformist regime, and, above all, it was unsuccessful in managing the modernization-developmental revolution that it had so enthusiastically initiated. Instead of spurring development—the raison d'être of the experiment—the regime retarded it and was not able to limit the role of foreign financial and investment capital. The reformist model failed to institutionalize inclusionary corporatism even if the change it initiated is irreversible.

This result reinforces our thesis that military praetorians whether oligarchic as in Nasser's Egypt or corporatist as in Peru since 1969, are incapable of creating viable and independent systems of collective behavior and of politics. They can only operate within organizational structures. (See, for example, the failure of the monstrous and complex but essentially fictional and ineffective structures that Nasser established between 1954 and 1961.) The

65. Alfred Stepan, *The State and Society: Peru in Comparative Perspective* (Princeton, N.J.: Princeton University Press, 1978), pp. 291–96.

military is a bureaucratic organization, not a political system. Notwithstanding the cases of the FAR and PLA, there is no way that the military establishment can conduct politics other than through bureaucratic and status politics. It can establish its corporate integrity, but it is unable to establish or even stimulate the creation of a political system and political vision. It is a superbureaucracy that in turn supervises bureaucratic structures; even here, however, the military has demonstrated poor administrative skills. It can be reformist or conservative, populist or reactionary, but its vision cannot include what makes politics work: autonomous and powerful social and political groups and structures. The military cannot create viable parties, parliaments, or pressure groups. It is skilled in executive performance but has no executive imagination. When it comes to politics, there are no troops. The military, as Collier has shown, can effect *policy*, not politics, and only limited modernization.

The military cannot command existing mobilization even if its reformist orientations demand it. Political mobilization calls for skills, experiences, and capabilities that are not learned or acquired by the modern corporate military establishment. Again, to speak of limited pluralism is to confuse elite circulation and cooptation with a more widespread collective political behavior. Limited pluralism, if it is a valid and verifiable theory, must refer to the existence of autonomous and independent political groups, of counterelites, and not to the formation of bureaucratic structures that are intended to be the basis for politics. It must demonstrate, in however limited a manner, that the system represents a multiplicity of interests and that there is a political process which revolves around conflicting sets of cross-cutting alliances, where bargaining and group accommodation occur.[66] None of this is even remotely likely in the policies of politics of any corporatist praetorian authoritarian regime. The political process inspired by the reformers in Peru stimulated activity at the local levels but this either withered or was harassed to death when it became threaten-

66. I borrowed the concept of limited pluralism from Jerry Hough, *The Soviet Union and Social Science Theory*, not because I accept it but because of Hough's interpretation of Soviet politics based on his misguided theory of limited pluralism.

ing to the dominant political groups. Repression stoppage—not political linkage—became the order of the day. Corporatism encourages patrimonial and clientalistic relationships, not pluralistic linkages, whether limited or otherwise.

The limits imposed on Latin America regimes are structural, institutional, and political. The resulting regimes are authoritarian, essentially praetorian, and preferably corporatist. Whether they are Marxist, reformist, radical, conservative, or reactionary, with the exception of Brazil and Argentina they are all modernizing, not developmental, regimes.

Authoritarianism is an orientation that is both cultural and structural. The ascendency of authoritarianism is related to perception of social behavior by the political elites (who are bureaucratic, technocratic, and militaristic) and to their instinct to dominate society by arresting or controlling collective behavior. On the whole, authoritarianism is predicated on damaging autonomous social and political behavior or on harnessing and encapsulating newly created social and economic groups. The degree of authoritarian intervention, and its success, depends on the efficiency of the authoritarian structures, not on the sensitivity or doubts that may creep into the authoritarian body politic or its elites. And it seems that the efficiency of military reformist authoritarian structures is not very impressive.

Authoritarianism is also a cultural predilection which has been found in Latin American political culture since independence. One does not have to be a cultural determinist in order to argue that authoritarianism, whether personalist, oligarchic, socialist, or radical, has persisted in Latin America since colonization. If these authoritarian regimes give way to nonauthoritarian systems, this author will be the first to recant. I do not foresee the decline of authoritarianism; the changes brought by modernization and economic development only enhance the structures of authoritarianism and help to create new types of authoritarian domination. Such a development was corporatism. This sytem prevailed in the Iberian Peninsula and has revived in Latin America since the 1940s. As an alternative to communism, socialism and fascism, the corporatist state is no stranger in the political environment of Catholic authoritarian systems. In fact, it is one of the major political conformations in Catholic modernizing policies. This does not mean that Sweden or England could not cultivate types of corporatism (British guild socialism, fabianism, and Swedish social democracy stand as counterexamples), but the political culture of Latin America is more receptive to the corporatist modernizing political system than are Protestant and nonauthoritarian political cultures.

Having said this, I insist that the civil-military dichotomy offered by several authors on Latin America is insufficient to explain the role of the military or, for that matter, the nature and purposes of regimes in Latin America.[67] Both civilian and military politicians in Latin America adopt authoritarian and corporatist orientations.[68] The military is probably more adept at administering and more inclined to institute a corporatist organic state than are, say, radical civilians who may prefer forms of socialist and communist developmentalism. Possible explanations for this are many (better or different education, different class origins, for instance), but they are insufficient. I have found no convincing argument in the literature on the military and politics in modern Latin America as to why the military is more radical and why the civilians are less radical.[69] The fact remains that bureaucrats, technocrats, and the military in Latin America usually prefer corporatist and organizational solutions to political problems.

Last, but not least, I insist on the validity of the praetorian explanation of the politics of corporatism and authoritarianism in Peru and other Latin American states.[70] Latin America's cultural, intellectual, and political commitments are demonstrated in the persistence of authoritarianism for over a century and of cor-

---

67. See John S. Fitch, "Radical Military Regimes in Latin America: Revolution, Rhetoric and Reality in Peru and Ecuador" (Paper delivered at American Political Science Association Convention, Washington, D.C., September 1977), pp. 1–32.

68. George Philip, "The Soldier as Radical: The Peruvian Military Government 1968–1975," *Latin American Studies* 8 (1976): 29–51.

69. Ibid., pp. 29–51.

70. Perlmutter, *Military and Politics in Modern Times*, pp. 166–205.

poratism since the 1940s. Here the distinction between civilian and military becomes an exercise in futility. Both groups frequently have adopted corporatism and they are certainly authoritarian.

I find that modern Iran under the Pahlavi regime did not possess the structures of modern authoritarianism and was not a modern authoritarian state. It was a patrimonial, classical autocracy. Politically and institutionally, there was nothing modern about the Shah's political system; it was an antipopulist regime. The Shah governed together with his family, the military, his sycophants, and their dependents, according to a classical Weberian concept of personal and traditional authority. No modern staff, no modern political structures or institutions with a mobilizational orientation nor any modern parallel institutions was established. More specifically, the Pahlavis did not create a single party, political police (the SAVAK was no different from secret police under Ivan the Terrible or Louis XIV; it was a personal instrument of the antipopulist Shah), autonomous military establishment, or auxiliary and parallel political structures. Iran's only modern elements were the techniques of economic modernization, the modern and sophisticated American-equipped military and the American-trained and -equipped police.

Superficially, the regime resembled a modernizing, not a developmental model. The Shah, like King Cyrus and the sultans, ruled on a personal basis. Relations with the senior military, the bureaucracy and the technocracy as well as their appointments were personalistic. The Shah suppressed both modern, liberal, pluralist forces and radical, reactionary, Islamic ones simultaneously. He prevented the emergence of *any* autonomous political expression or organization whether authoritarian, Marxist, liberal or Islamic. With the military his base of his support, he prevented the emergence of a general staff in order to keep the separate army, navy, and air force branches from becoming autonomous, and he personally controlled his army chiefs as well as the bureaucracies and capitalists. The White Revolution in the countryside was dominated and directed by the Shah.

The Shah's personal regime approximated oriental, but not modern, despotism. Thus, when it was threatened he had no auxiliary and parallel structures to rely upon. He had no party to employ the police, no youth groups, and no movement or ideology to rally the masses against the Ayatollahs, who successfully mobilized them. The Shah, who did not rule a modern authoritarian state, was oblivious to the uses of mass mobilization and manipulation and hoped to rule by virtue of personal despotism and a personal police. Therefore, he could only mobilize the military and directly confront the people. No contemporary ruler can do this successfully in a country of thirty-six million people that has a relatively advanced and modernizing economic system. The Shah's abdication, unlike the Czar's, brought about the collapse of the military, the personal police, and the dependent bureaucracy. This is not conducive to sultanism and oriental despotism. A dictatorship without complementary popular political structures cannot survive because it is not a modern, rational (in the Weberian sense) political system. The Shah's regime was reformist; in fact, its reforms surpassed most praetorian reformist regimes (those of Egypt and Syria, for example). But the system was also patrimonial. The politically unorganized forces it had unleashed but failed to restrain with efficient, modern authoritarian political structures were its undoing. The Pahlavi system was neither ideological nor mobilizational; Iran was not a modern authoritarian state.

CHAPTER FOUR

Conclusion

Ideology and Organization

Ideology sustains and helps to institutionalize authoritarian political structures. Thus highly institutionalized authoritarian regimes exploit ideology, while in noninstitutionalized regimes ideology is vague or fails to serve the purposes of organizational structures. The failure of corporatist and praetorian regimes is an organizational-ideological failure; neither type of regime can command ideological commitment, and neither has turned ideology into organizationally and politically successful arrangements. As a result, such modern authoritarian ideologies as radical nationalism, anticosmopolitanism, anticolonialism and antiliberalism, serve only as negative political values and are used to eliminate political and ethnic rivals. Corporatist and praetorian regimes cannot mobilize social forces to achieve a stable political order, because their organization has no relation to ideology.

Because praetorianism and the new corporatism are neither ideologies nor political movements, they remain disturbing and divisive forces in society and politics. They are types of regimes and primarily societal arrangements. The old corporatism was a movement with an ideology which failed because it refused to establish modern authoritarian structures such as the single party and because its ideology was not an integrating force. The old corporatist ideology was based on a resuscitated Thomistic concept of society which could not cope with the modern world. It refused to accept modernism but aspired to circumvent the modern

174

ideologies imbued in communism and fascism; it therefore collapsed in Spain and Portugal as soon as Franco and Salazar were dead.

When one speaks of "totalitarianism," one means an institutionalized authoritarian regime sustained by a combination of organization and ideology. Institutionalized authoritarian regimes have an ideological orientation; noninstitutionalized authoritarian regimes are basically nonideological. In fact, the commitment to a developmental model could not be achieved solely by pragmatically and technically oriented bureaucracies. These bureaucracies must be supervised, so to speak, not by super-bureaucracies such as the corporatist and praetorian executives, but by political structures—the party, the propaganda machinery, the auxiliary structures such as youth movements, and a politicized (ideologized) police. Totalitarianism, whose raison d'être, however forgotten or neglected, was ideological, does not serve as an explanation of modern authoritarian regimes. It certainly does not help us to distinguish between institutionalized and noninstitutionalized modern authoritarianism.

Nationalist and racist ideologies can and did mobilize social forces, but alone they cannot sustain regimes. Both ideology and organization or an organizational ideology that can mobilize social forces and sustain the political order are essential to the survival of regimes, as Gregor clearly demonstrates in his studies of Italian fascism.[1] Nationalism is one of the most effective ideological symbols exploited by developmental regimes because it can be used to extract social and natural resources in the pursuit of modernization. Yet, nationalist aspirations and commitments cannot substitute for the ethos of work, sacrifice, and frugality, which is necessary for the success of a developmental program. Nationalism, though an ideology of delayed industrialization, cannot organize, lift, and sustain a modern regime and cannot encourage and regulate extractive enterprise. Nor is a nationalist ideology sufficient to transform the dynamics of development into a political order because it neither rewards entrepreneurial, managerial, or leadership

1. A. James Gregor, *Italian Fascism and Developmental Dictatorship* (Princeton, N.J.: Princeton University Press, 1979).

skills nor encompasses a set of beliefs appropriate to the creation of a new order. In this respect it resembles religion; both can mobilize social groups and human forces, but alone neither can organize or manage the mobilization of social resources.

Like nationalism, Marxism and fascism provide inadequate guidelines for political action that effectively institutes political order. Both ideologies, infused into organizational structures like the party and the youth movement, can establish political order only during the revolutionary and developmental process. Political ideology tends to become a product of governmental and institutional policies rather than an innovative force therein. Contrary to the tenets of classical Marxism, the state and its political structures and organizations sustain Marxist ideology; ideology does not sustain the state.

The failure of reformist, praetorian, and other forms of noninstitutionalized authoritarianism is connected with the failure either to successfully execute the functions of institutionalized authoritarianism or to establish a true authoritative political elite such as the communists have. The success of communist authoritarianism is connected with the linkage between ideology and organization. Ideology became an organizational weapon, and the organizational machinery came to be dominated by a political elite (in the case of China and Cuba it is recruited from the military).[2]

The single ideological and totalitarian party, its auxiliary instruments, and the propaganda and ideological networks are necessary to initiate and sustain developmental authoritarianism. The experiences of Egypt and Peru clearly demonstrate that the failure of the reformists can be traced to the relationship between ideology and organizational structure.[3] Nasser and his Free Offi-

2. For an extensive analysis of ideology and organization, see P. Selznick, *The Organizational Weapon* (New York: Free Press, 1952); Franz Schurmann, *Ideology and Organization in Communist China* (Berkeley: University of California Press, 1966); and Amos Perlmutter, "Ideology and Organization: The Socialist-Zionist Movement" (Ph.D. diss., University of California, Berkeley, 1957).

3. For Egypt, see Baker, *Egypt's Uncertain Revolution under Nasser and Sadat* (Cambridge, Mass.: Harvard University Press, 1978); and P. J. Vatikiotis, *Nasser and His Generation* (London: Croom Helm, 1978). For Peru, see Alfred Stepan, *State and Society: Peru in Comparative Perspective*

cers Corps opted for an Egyptian revolution to be carried out by the
military. After a decade of failure, Nasser hesitantly decided in
1962 to establish a political, rather than a bureaucratic,
instrument—the Arab Socialist Union—to project the revolution. It
was designed to separate the military from the machinery of reform and the reform from the administrative structure. Once
again, he failed. Nasser was not fully committed to an experiment (the ASU) that would diminish his political power and
create an alternative political elite even if he had wanted the
ASU to take political power from the military establishment.
Thus, he failed to establish an organization imbued with a revolutionary ideology and instead used a nationalist and pan-Arabist
ideology to make his praetorian and authoritarian rule more effective.[4] In this case, ideology did not buttress the revolutionary organization, but Nasser hoped it would help sustain authoritarianism.

The Peruvian military's effort to achieve autonomy so that it
could implement a successful reform created a wedge, rather than
a link, between the newly created social groups and the military.
The military program, or its autonomous behavior, separated it
from the old, oligarchic classes. Not wanting to ally themselves
with a specific socioeconomic class, and maintaining a distance
from newly created interest groups, the military exhibited a certain ideological ambiguity.[5] What resulted is referred to in Peru as
Hermetismo: "the military—and generally *only* the military—made
final key decisions in their private closed quarters, 'hermetically
sealed' from potentially important civilian output."[6]

Egyptian and Peruvian procedures were military in style: they
were indifferent to or suspicious of the link between revolutionary
ideology and the military organization. This, paradoxically, followed the concept Lenin adopted from Clausewitz, which is that

(Princeton, N.J.: Princeton University Press, 1978); and C. McClintock "The
Ambiguity of Peru's Third Way: Costs and Benefits" (Paper delivered at
Wilson Center workshop on "The Peruvian Experiment Reconsidered,"
Washington, D.C., November 2–4, 1978).

4. Baker, *Egypt's Uncertain Revolution* is an excellent exposition of the
Nasserists' dilemma.
5. McClintock, "The Ambiguity of Peru's Third Way," pp. 9–11.
6. Ibid., p. 10.

the party, like the army, is a mobilizational organization run by the general staff of the revolution—the professional revolutionary elite. Lenin, the master revolutionary, clearly understood that ambiguity is fatal for revolutionary ideology, organization, and commitment. The praetorian, oligarchic, and corporatist search for a third way which is neither communist nor capitalist enhanced noninstitutional political authoritarianism but not political and economic developmentalism.

The Quintessence of Modern Authoritarianism

It has been over three decades since the collapse of nazism and fascism. Three quarters of a century has passed since the Bolshevik Revolution, and the bolshevik model, however modified, is still with us. Latin American corporatist praetorianism has a century-long history, and we have seen over three decades of Arab-Moslem oligarchic praetorianism and close to two decades of African despotic praetorianism.

Accumulated experience makes a revisionist approach to the concepts of modern authoritarianism and totalitarianism necessary. Because of new, though unbalanced, documentation (there is abundant documentation for nazism, fascism, and bolshevism; little for Latin American, Arab-Moslem and African praetorianism, although there is a great deal of analysis) and the passage of time since the horrors of the Lenin-Stalin gulags and Hitler's gas chambers, we must begin reassessing traditional approaches, myths, and ideologically influenced interpretations of this century's most remarkable political phenomenon: authoritarianism/totalitarianism.

This tour d'horizon has sketched and critically reassessed the phenomenon of modern authoritarianism—its varieties, typologies, and dynamics. The theme has dictated a focus upon politics in the classical Aristotelian sense, even though extensive investigation of the social and economic causes of the phenomenon is imperative. In my view, the ideological explanations have been overdone; there are more books and essays written on the ideological-totalitarian aspect of the phenomenon than on any other. This is only natural, of course, since most of the totalitarian literature was written between thirty and fifty years ago while nazism, fascism, and bolshevism were still developing and when information was scanty and unreliable. Thus, in its time, Koestler's *Darkness at Noon* was as revealing as Solzhenitsyn's *The Gulag Archipelago* is at present. In addition, cultural historians, ideological Marxists, and democratic liberals were attracted to explaining the phenomenon in ideological-philosophical, historiosophic, and metaphysical terms. I have chosen to concentrate on the key signposts that political scientists, political theorists, and students of comparative history and politics can observe. This analysis has led to the following conclusions.

1. Modern authoritarianism, with the possible exception of the party-state in the USSR, is *not* a totalitarian movement, party, or regime. In the most basic sense, the relationships and interactions between the structures (elites, the state, the party, parallel and auxiliary structures, and the mass society) and forces of authoritarianism are authoritarian or autocratic rather than totalitarian. I distinguish political authoritarianism from metaphysical, existential, and historiosophic totalitarianism, and I use the former concept to describe the varying relationships between the despot, the regime, the parallel and auxiliary structures, the party, and the state and within each. Authoritarianism is based on the intervention of auxiliary instruments into all aspects of life—private, group, religious, social, economic, and political. The only modern authoritarianism that approximates a total form is the bolshevik party-state. The absence of organized collective behavior and the penetration of the party and the state into the society guarantee the stability of bolshevik authoritarianism.

2. Modern authoritarianism is distinguished from other authoritarian regimes by the linkage and interaction—however unequal—between the despot, the ruling elite, the regime, the state, the party, parallel and auxiliary structures, and the masses. In other words, modern authoritarianism is the authoritarianism of mass movements. Modern politics have produced political mobilization and a revolution in the nature and extent of political participation; this mobilization forces rulers and regimes to adopt developmental attitudes. Modernization and change require new types of extractive and regulative structures, which are the **parallel**

and auxiliary political structures that were unknown under classical tyranny or medieval despotism. Political mobilization has linked rulers, however despotic their orientation might be, to the people.

There are also two traditional political elements that are relevant to the rise, survival, or fall of all modern dictatorships. One is the absence of societal political demands for natural rights, freedoms, and political pluralism, and the other is the existence of a mass society. No modern authoritarian system, with the possible exception of Cuba, has successfully achieved the consensus of the masses or has adequately represented its aspirations. At best, the mass society has been exploited. Since the ability of an authoritarian regime to stay in power and govern depends on how the dictator or his closest supporters manipulate the regime, the elites, the state, the party, and *organized* social forces and interests, no dictatorship has ever been established through the broad and open mobilization of the mass society. From its inception, the Bolshevik regime, though calling itself the dictatorship of the proletariat, practiced a highly restrictive form of mobilization that excluded large segments of the peasantry, the intellectuals, and the working classes. In fact, the major function of all modern authoritarians is to limit political mobilization and assign the representation of various groups' interests to functional, bureaucratic elites. The major objective of the modern dictatorship is to institutionalize itself, if necessary by paying lip service to the need for political mobilization or by using whatever modern and dynamic forces are available to legitimize and sustain itself. When an authoritarian system relies on mass mobilization, it does so only in order to destroy the centers of socioeconomic power that lie outside the state system. Even then, this mobilization is channeled through the state elites. The three major totalitarian movements of modern times began as small coteries and ended as corporate, minority-dominated entities.

3. The major purpose of a modern dictatorship or, for that matter, any tyranny, is to achieve a political monopoly over all forces, groups, classes, interests, and structures within the system. The most successful innovation for this purpose is obviously the single party. Thus, the degree of authoritarianism, its extension of power,

and its sustenance depends upon how successfully the modern dictatorship cultivates this type of party.

The stability of the dictatorship depends on how well it exploits the party in order to establish political control and on the success and flexibility with which the party dominates the elites, the state, and the opposition. In the Bolshevik case, the party-state is dominant. In the Nazi case, the despot successfully exploited party-state rivalries in order to dominate both of them. Mussolini unsuccessfully tried to act as an arbiter between the party and the state. He failed to dominate the bureaucracy, the elites, or the party because neither the party nor the state was effectively institutionalized. The test of a durable dictatorship is its ability to govern the leading elites that control the masses by means of the party and the political police. In the communist system, auxiliary and parallel structures are essential for the dictator to maintain control. In Nazi Germany, the auxiliary and parallel structures declined, but the despot survived and continued to dominate the party, the state, and the society through the use of charisma, propaganda, and instruments of terror. In Fascist Italy, the despot, who had no institutionalized political or auxiliary structures and lacked an alternative power base, governed with the support of the state, the corporate council, the Fascist youth movement, the army, and the syndicates. But he could not claim any one of them as his single source of support.

4. The authoritarian state is the archetypal modern centralized state. Its political structures are hegemonic in orientation and its rulers are monopolistic elites vying for power among the oligopolistic political structures. The modern authoritarian state is oriented toward grand organizations, and its most effective instruments are political and economic bureaucratic structures.

5. The sine qua non of the relatively stable and successful party-state dictatorships of modern times—communism, nazism, and fascism—is the subordination of the professional military and the revolutionary-militia to the civilian political dictatorship. This is done by relying on the help of the single party, the state, or the professional military. No mobilizational dictatorship will tolerate either hegemonic rule by the military or dependence upon them as

the sole source of political support and legitimation, but the military does have a symbiotic relationship with the party in several communist regimes.

Under nonrevolutionary dictatorships, both the military and the state are noninstitutionalized and therefore unstable. No instrument exists to subordinate the military. No praetorian dictatorship has at its disposal even a fragmented party. At best, the oligarchic praetorian will create or harness an existing radical nationalist or popular party, which guarantees the oligarchy greater longevity than does dependence upon a single despotic, praetorian party. However, without exception, no type of praetorianism, including a corporate praetorian dictatorship, can survive without the support of the military establishment.

Praetorian tyrannical or oligarchic regimes are nonmobilizational, permanently unstable, and noninstitutionalized. The corporate praetorian regime, which is sustained by a coalition of the military, managers, technocrats, and bureaucrats, has a greater chance of survival as long as the military establishment is cohesive and the other members of the coalition refrain from disrupting it.

Nevertheless, the cohesiveness of the military in the corporate-praetorian regime is not a sufficiently powerful political force to sustain a corporatist regime. The corporatist alliance also needs to be balanced. In this case, the military acts as an arbitrator between the different corporate structures. The inequality of the corporatist structures with the military's privileged position guarantees the praetorian regime in corporatist systems. Modernization and mobilization further enhance the possibility of corporate praetorian domination. Thus, modernizing populism and corporatism in Latin America both promote praetorianism and authoritarianism.

Military intervention would arouse divisiveness and probably lead to the destruction of authoritarian praetorian rule, probably in favor of another version. Edward Shils wrote some time ago that in a military oligarchy the gap between the modernizing elite and the population is wide. "To summarize: the military oligarchy is not a complete regime. It has neither a comprehensive program nor a perspective into the future."[7]

7. Edward Shils, "The Military in the Political Development of the

6. The institutionalization of a modern authoritarian regime may be guided by an individual, a party, a state corporate oligarchy, or the military. One of them must ultimately achieve a hegemonic role in supporting the dictatorship. There is no political space for a balanced pluralist equilibrium, as advanced by some Soviet and Latin American scholars. Political and bureaucratic control over the party or the state is the Communists' most effective method of consolidating the dictatorship. However, one should not confuse political institutionalization with the consolidation of the dictatorship even though they are complementary political activities and often represent parallel efforts. Bureaucratic control also safeguards against the decline of parallel and auxiliary structures and of the single, monopolistic party. The function of the politicized police in institutionalized systems and of the military in noninstitutionalized systems is of primary importance in preserving the regime.

7. Mannheim and other intellectual antirevolutionaries argue that the politics of a mass society involves "the loss of exclusiveness of elites and the rise of mass participation in cultural and political life."[8] Arendt's school contends that it means "the loss of an insulation of non-elites and the rise of elites bent on total mobilization of a population."[9] If one accepts these definitions, the only mass society is Bolshevik Russia and, to a lesser extent, Nazi Germany. In fact, the outstanding characteristic of modern authoritarian regimes is their failure to conform to either school's existential concept of the mass society, a convenient but inaccurate and nonempirical concept. If "*mass society* requires both accessible elites and available non-elites," then it is no more than a general statement of conditions existing in all modern politics, not only in authoritarian and totalitarian systems.[10]

Instead of inventing vague and oversimplified terms, one

New States," in *The Role of the Military in Underdeveloped Countries*, ed. J. S. Johnson (Princeton, N.J.: Princeton University Press, 1962), pp. 7–67.

8. William Kornhauser, *The Politics of Mass Society* (New York: Free Press, 1959), pp. 21–23. Quote is from p. 21.

9. Ibid., p. 22.

10. Ibid., p. 41.

should examine the political dynamics of the mass society in the authoritarian context in order to understand the politics of modern authoritarianism. "Availability" or "nonavailability" of elites and nonelites does not explain the institutional, instrumental, procedural, and political behavior of modern authoritarianism. It can be argued that authoritarian societies are molded by a few elites, but that the focus of such regimes in modern times is not so much on masses, classes, or groups, but on political instruments, that is, on the institutional and procedural arrangements that facilitate authoritarianism.

These instruments of control, at the disposal of the monopolistic elites, are used to dominate the state and thereby the society, the party, and the corporate council. Indeed, in authoritarian systems, the few rule the many who do not have political rights and freedoms. Thus, the most basic statement on modern authoritarianism need not be clouded by resorting to vague concepts of elites and nonelites.

8. The role of ideology generally and of totalitarian ideology specifically in modern authoritarianism has been left until last. I do not think anyone would seriously challenge the statement that all regimes in all times and all places are ruled in the name of some ideology: in both open and closed political systems, whoever rules does so in the name of ideology. It is also true that the twentieth century is a century of ideologies. In a relatively short period of time, an unparalleled number of divergent and militant ideologies have emerged—bolshevism, nazism, fascism, futurism, racism, syndicalism, and integral nationalism.

The ideologues who rose to prominence in the twentieth century all shared a desire or mission to annihilate pluralist liberal and democratic ideas, institutions, and regimes. The survival of *all* modern authoritarian, totalitarian, and autocratic regimes is dependent not so much on their ideological commitment, purity, and zealotry, as on their ability to successfully orchestrate the party, the state, the parallel and auxiliary structures, and the society in the direction of authoritarianism. Variation in the efficiency of such tools of modern authoritarianism as the single party, the political police, propaganda, youth movements, squadristi, the **SA** and SS, the Red Guards, the military, and the bureaucracy ex-

plains the dynamics and political nature of modern authoritarianism more accurately than grand theories and his-
toriosophical explanations. Ideological constructs cannot explain
the political differences between one authoritarian system and
another; an examination of the types of political structures and instruments is necessary.

Thus, although the Fascists created new forms of aggressive and
authoritarian nationalism, racism, and metaphysical ideologies,
and though the Bolsheviks ushered in the most efficient ideological
party-state of all time, both inaugurated new types of structures
and instruments of monopolistic domination. The annihilation of
liberalism, democratic socialism, democracy, and parliamentarism
was achieved by these new instruments, not by the inexorable
march of totalitarian ideology.

In no way can ideological analysis explain the sustenance, survival, or decay of the authoritarian political system. *Only when
wedded to political organization does ideology become an instrument
of power and a useful explanatory tool.* It can offer brilliant explanations for the beginnings of bolshevism, nazism, and fascism;
however, the survival and sustenance of all modern authoritarian
models is explained by their innovative use of the monopolistic
party and its auxiliary and parallel structures to manipulate mass
societies. In fact, the ideology of modern authoritarianism is derived from the institutional and political arrangements of these
political systems rather than the reverse. This is unquestionably
true of corporatism and praetorianism. The raison d'être of authoritarian rule in the communist and fascist models was derived
more from political power than from ideology.

The continued existence of each authoritarian type depends on
the degree, scope, and level of autocratic measures and arrangements, not on the quality of ideology, totalitarian or otherwise. The
more politically developed the oligarchic instruments, the better
the chances an authoritarian system will survive. The survival of
the modern mass type of restrictive tyranny must be explained in
terms of political dynamics, structural innovations, elite domination, and the struggle for legitimation and for the maintenance of
political stability. Ideology and totalitarianism can at best explain
the origin of only a few movements, and even these could have sur-

vived politically without them. Thus, the Lenin-Stalin system needed the gulag state; Hitler, the Final Solution; Mussolini, the Mare Nostrum; the praetorians, their nationalistic mumbo-jumbo; and the corporatists, the harmonious ideology that justifies the newly established authoritarian structures that sustain the regime. Ideology did not legitimize such regimes any more than the decline of ideology robbed them of their legitimacy. Modern tyranny and authoritarianism, unlike historical tyrannies, constantly confront the problem of legitimacy. After all, in the age of the mass society and the explosion of political mobilization, in an age caught up in a revolution of political participation, the modern authoritarian system depends on the ability of political institutions to mobilize the support of the mass societies. Authoritarians have not succeeded in legitimizing their rule yet, except through coercion of the mass electorate. Thus far it is the political monopoly of the ruling elite(s) over the party, the state, the corporate council, and the society that explains why modern authoritarian systems are still with us after close to a century of brutal rule.

Index

Africa, North, 80, 124. *See also* Middle East

Africa, sub-Saharan, 15, 24, 41, 42, 82, 134, 148, 163, 178

Agitation, 73, 74; propaganda distinguished from, 22–23, 107

Agitprop machinery, 17, 143

Allen, William S., 64

Allende, Salvador, 134

Amin, Idi, 41, 134

Anti-Semitism, *see* Ideology

Antonescu, Ion, 27

Arab regimes, *see* Middle East

Arab Socialist Union (ASU), 148, 150, 151, 177

Arendt, Hannah, 63, 64, 65, 68, 95, 183

Argentina, 85, 125, 151, 156, 161, 167; corporatism/praetorianism in, 63, 80, 117, 132–34, 152–54, 170. *See also* Latin America

Aristotle, 84, 178

Army, *see* Military, the

Assad, Hafez al-, 75, 134, 149

Ataturk, Kemal, 52, 75, 126

Austria: corporatism in, 117, 119

Austro-Hungarian Empire, 107

Authoritarianism, modern: civil-military relations under, *see* Military, the; vs. classical, 120; defined and analyzed, 24, 179–86; development of, 30–31, 136–73; dynamics of, xiii, 10, 24, 44–50 passim, 62, 66, 89–135, 136–56, 184; institutionalized, 5–6, 13, 17, 22, 58, 137–47, 157, 161–62, 175, 183; models, types, and political structures of, 9, 24, 28–51, 89–135; non-institutionalized, 5, 13, 147–73, 175–76; political behavior of, 7–28, 50; requirements for, 67–69, 120–21; time sequences in, 44, 46–48

Autocracy, 12; classical/traditional, 26, 49, 120; defined, 1; modern military, 15, 130. *See also* Police, political; Praetorianism

Autonomy: military, 52–55, 60–61; of modern state, 2–4, 8. *See also* Military, the

Auxiliary structures, 9–16, 28, 64, 65, 132–35, 181; fascist, 111–14; function of, 18; nazi, 96, 98–107; parties as, 24; in seizure of power, xii, 12, 16–22, 73, 126; soviet, 94–95, 98; three types of,

Le Bon, Gustave, 78
Legitimacy, political, xii, 10, 11,
    17–19, 118, 121, 129, 166
Lenin, V. I., 16, 22, 55, 82, 84,
    89–93, 177, 178, 186; and Len-
    ninism, 14, 47, 51, 53, 66, 68, 78,
    91; party and party-state of, 17,
    50, 74–77, 97; propaganda use
    by, 23, 72; and totalitarianism,
    65–66, 69; *What Is To Be Done?*,
    77
LeoGrande, William, 54, 60, 61, 71
Ley, Robert, 34, 105
Libya, 10, 87
Lin Piao, 47, 53
Linz, Juan J., 65–70 passim, 120,
    121, 122, 161, 162
Locke, John, 50
Lowenthal, Richard, 140, 143
Luxemburg, Rosa, 82
Lyttleton, Adrian, 82, 112

Maier, Charles, 115
Malloy, James, 151, 153
Mannheim, Karl, 183
Mao Tse-tung and Maoism, 16, 22,
    23, 46, 50–56 passim, 66–71
    passim, 84, 85; messianism of, 63
Marx, Karl, 56, 79, 90; and Mar-
    xism, xi, 4, 5, 23, 53, 68, 72, 81,
    87, 92, 143, 176; Marxism-
    fascism relationship, 75–78,
    107–09, 146
McClintock, Cynthia, 168
Mexico, 122. *See also* Latin
    America
Michels, Roberto, 77, 113
Middle East: Arab regimes in, 15,
    24, 41, 82, 85, 87, 108, 124, 133–
    34, 163, 178; praetorianism in,
    80, 82, 85, 124, 133, 148. *See also
    individual countries*
Military, the, 1, 19, 62, 81, 84–85;
    bolshevism and, 91–92; and
    bureaucratic authoritarianism,

125, 127–28; civil-military rela-
    tions, 41–44, 51–53, 89, 115–16,
    128–35, 149–51, 155, 166–71
    passim, 177; coups d'etat, 19, 52,
    80, 85, 129; as elite, 7, 11, 59,
    61–62, 122–23, 159–60, 176; Hi-
    tler and, 30, 51, 52, 98–99, 100–
    04, 138; modern autocracies, 15,
    130; and party-army symbiosis,
    14, 47, 53–62, 93, 148, 160–61,
    181–82; in Spain, 120–21
Mills, C. Wright, 141
Minoritarianism, 76, 78, 82
Mobilization, political, 11, 15–18,
    26, 30–31, 68–69, 180; bolshevik,
    90–94; corporatist, 38, 132–33;
    fascist, 109–11; in Latin America,
    118, 164; the military and, 169;
    nazi, 96; of peasantry, 86, 159–
    60. *See also* Seizure of power
Mobutu, Joseph, 41, 134
Monarchy/monarchism, 3, 27, 110,
    111; and monarchical tyranny,
    80, 82. *See also* Tyranny
Montesquieu, Charles Louis de, 3, 4
Mosca, Gaetano, 113
Mussolini, Benito, 23, 65, 66, 72,
    75–78, 82, 84, 108; and cor-
    poratism, 30, 74, 112–13, 162;
    and empire (Mare Nostrum), 79,
    112–13, 186; Hitler's demands
    on, 85, 86; and party/party-state,
    17, 18, 110–11, 137, 181; social
    reforms of, 145–47. *See also* Fas-
    cist movement

Nasser, Gamal Abdel, 65, 81, 163–
    64, 167; failure of, 50, 75, 134,
    148, 150, 154–55, 158–59, 165–66,
    176–77; praetorianism/corpor-
    atism of, 10, 15, 70, 74, 75,
    82–85 passim, 124, 150–51, 168
Nationalism, *see* Ideology
National Socialist party, 15, 29,
    144